WAYNE
and
FORD

Also by Nancy Schoenberger

Dangerous Muse: The Life of Lady Caroline Blackwood

WITH SAM KASHNER

*Furious Love: Elizabeth Taylor, Richard Burton,
and the Marriage of the Century*

*Hollywood Kryptonite: The Bulldog, the Lady,
and the Death of Superman*

A Talent for Genius: The Life and Times of Oscar Levant

POETRY

Long Like a River

Girl on a White Porch

The Taxidermist's Daughter

WAYNE
and
FORD

The Films,
the Friendship,
and the
Forging of an
American Hero

Nancy Schoenberger

NAN A. TALESE

Doubleday

New York   London   Toronto   Sydney   Auckland

Copyright © 2017 by Nancy Schoenberger

All rights reserved. Published in the United States by Nan A. Talese/Doubleday,
a division of Penguin Random House LLC, New York, and distributed
in Canada by Random House of Canada, a division of Penguin Random House
Canada Limited, Toronto.

www.nanatalese.com

DOUBLEDAY is a registered trademark of Penguin Random House LLC.
Nan A. Talese and the colophon are trademarks of Penguin Random House LLC.

All material quoted from the John Ford Papers courtesy of
the Lilly Library at Indiana University, Bloomington.

All photographs courtesy of Photofest.

Book design by Maria Carella
Jacket design by Michael J. Windsor
Front-of-jacket photographs courtesy of the Everett Collection
Back-of-jacket image © James Steid/Shutterstock

Library of Congress Cataloging-in-Publication Data
Names: Schoenberger, Nancy.
Title: Wayne and Ford : the films, the friendship, and the forging of an
American hero / Nancy Schoenberger.
Description: First edition. | New York : Nan A. Talese Doubleday, 2017. |
Includes bibliographical references and index.
Identifiers: LCCN 2016057903 | ISBN 9780385534857 (hardcover) |
ISBN 9780385534864 (ebook)
Subjects: LCSH: Ford, John, 1894–1973—Criticism and interpretation. |
Wayne, John, 1907–1979—Criticism and interpretation. |
Western films—History and criticism.
Classification: LCC PN1998.3.F65 S36 2017 | DDC 791.4302/33092—dc23
LC record available at https://lccn.loc.gov/2016057903

MANUFACTURED IN THE UNITED STATES OF AMERICA

1 3 5 7 9 10 8 6 4 2

First Edition

For Lieutenant Commander
Sigmund Bernard "Dutch" Schoenberger,

PILOT, FATHER, WESTERN FAN,

1923–2006

✳

Contents

WAYNE
and
FORD

Prologue:
Why Westerns Still Matter

John Ford and John Wayne taught us how to be men.
—JOHN MILIUS

I've played the kind of man I'd like to have been.
—JOHN WAYNE

Why do I love Westerns? Maybe I like to see men trying to do the right thing, often against tremendous odds and often for the protection of women and children, who are frequently as tough and feisty as the men who do the actual fighting. Though mostly written by men for men, the Western lays claim to anyone who loves storytelling because it is an inherently dramatic form—usually a quest narrative that follows the hero's progression from innocence to experience, ignorance to knowledge, shame to redemption, outcast to community. Sometimes the trajectory is reversed, a fall from grace. These are all human journeys. They transcend any one demographic.

As a fan of Westerns, I'm not alone among women. And despite historian Garry Wills's observation that "It is easy to see why so few women are fans of John Wayne," a handful of women writers have written encomiums to the stoic, sometimes bullying, sometimes tender archetypal hero embodied by Duke Wayne; writers such as Joan Didion, film critic Molly Haskell, and *New York Times* columnists Maureen Dowd and Alessandra Stanley have described their appreciation of Westerns and of one Western star in particular: John "Duke" Wayne, born Marion Morrison in Winterset, Iowa, in 1907.

"When John Wayne rode through my childhood, and perhaps through yours, he determined forever the shape of certain of our dreams," wrote Didion in 1965 after visiting the set of *The Sons of Katie Elder*, a Western starring Wayne directed by Henry Hathaway. Amazingly, it was Wayne's 136th picture, and he would go on to make 17 more. In a piece titled "John Wayne, a Love Story" for the *Saturday Evening Post*, she recalled the first time she saw Wayne on-screen, in the summer of 1943: "Saw the walk, heard the voice. Heard him tell the girl in a picture called *War of the Wildcats* that he would build her a house 'at the bend in the river where the cottonwoods grow.'" That line of dialogue has haunted her, she writes, a bit wistfully; it is "still the line I wait to hear."

In 1976, Molly Haskell visited the set of John Wayne's last film, *The Shootist*, in which he plays an aging gunfighter, John Bernard Books, who is dying of cancer. As sometimes happens with actors who become icons in their own time, the movie's universe merged with reality: in 1964, cancer had claimed one of John Wayne's lungs, and the strength and vitality for which he had been justly celebrated was noticeably diminished. In "Wayne, Westerns, and Women," Haskell writes of her visit to the Burbank, California, set: "I am here because I consider Wayne one of the great movie actors of all time—a view not universally held among my fellow film critics." She describes identifying with masculine movie heroes—instead of their wives or sweethearts—when she and her friends were tree-climbing tomboys: "We rode the range and slept under the stars and shot bad guys with the best of the men." It was an unwelcome revelation as she matured that she was supposed to identify not with the male hero but with "the little woman" keeping the turf fires burning at home on the prairie—a revelation I shared as I entered my own teenage years.

For Haskell, Wayne evolved from role model in youth to, on one level, "the father figure who has come home to us, the father who will make, has made, the world safe for us so that we may explore and find ourselves." Noting how audiences in the mid-1970s abandoned the Western, Haskell goes on to declare her appreciation of the Western hero as embodied by John Wayne:

> [He] was paternal without being a patriarch; he was involved in an action cinema that concentrated on male friendships but he was not a symbol of *machismo*. If we didn't desert him, it was because he didn't desert us. He never seemed to be fleeing the grasp of a woman, the strings of domesticity. Often his quest was motivated by a woman, by some great love. And the fact that he wasn't a ladies' man, a womanizer who winked at every passing dame, made him more attractive.

When his character does pursue a woman, Wayne "doesn't immediately see her in terms of her sexual possibilities, doesn't force her into a romantic mold to satisfy male fantasy." As Haskell notes, Wayne was usually paired with mature women, not starlets—Maureen O'Hara, Patricia Neal, Colleen Dewhurst, Katharine Hepburn. "He doesn't need sweet young things to bolster his ego," Haskell writes. "Wayne has had the most startlingly rich and sensual relationships with mature women." Wayne is masculine but not macho, which she aptly defines as "sexual arrogance and preening, excesses of masculinity that come at a time when the real thing—functional masculinity that Wayne represents—is disappearing."

Indeed, the scene in which Wayne first sees Maureen O'Hara as Mary Kate Danaher strolling barefoot through a pasture in her red skirt and blue apron in John Ford's *The Quiet Man* is a purely lyrical moment of romantic recognition. And in *The Searchers*, his doomed, unspoken love for his sister-in-law, Martha Edwards, adds a layer of pathos to the hero's quest to find his niece, kidnapped by the Comanches.

∗

John Wayne particularly resonates with me. You might call it my "John Wayne problem." You see, I grew up with men like Ford and Wayne; not only did my father look like John Wayne, but as a career military officer and a test pilot he lived the code of masculinity that John Ford and John Wayne created and embodied throughout the films, especially the Westerns, they made together. We all know that code, because, for good or for ill, it shaped America's ideal of masculinity, what it means to "be a man": to bear adversity in silence, to show courage in the face of fear, to bond with other men, to put honor and country before self—in three words, "stoicism," "courage," "duty." John Wayne came to embody those virtues on-screen, and men like my father embodied them in life.

When my father's test pilot buddies came over to the house, it was an alcohol-fueled, machismo-fest of swaggering men who loved their work, their families, and each other. What men like my father knew of America, they learned, in part, from John Ford. What they knew about being men, they learned from John Wayne. I remember taking long, cross-country trips with my family—all six of us kids bundled into the backseat of a maroon Packard—traveling through "Ford Country": the red plateaus and majestic rock formations of Monument Valley, the Navajo reservations of southern Utah. My father conveyed to us the idea that America's vast landscapes were sacred, an idea conveyed to him, and made iconic for him, by John Ford Westerns.

Today, the idea of "traditional masculinity" may seem old-fashioned. After all, this is an era of gender fluidity, one that is finally removing age-old stigmas against LGBT culture. Wayne and Ford's male archetype may seem trapped behind a nostalgia-tinted lens, and some argue it no longer even exists. "Masculin-

ity is just becoming something that is imitated from the movies,"
feminist writer Camille Paglia said in a 2013 online interview for
the *Wall Street Journal*. She pointed to the undervaluing of the
military—traditionally an all-male enclave—and the decline of
America's industrial base as evidence that masculinity has become
endangered in modern times. "There's nothing left. There's no
room for anything manly right now," she argued, in part because
men are left with "no models of manhood."

But the idea of learning how to "be a man" still has relevance
to all of us, born male or female. At their best, the qualities
and attributes that make men men, at least in John Ford–John
Wayne Westerns, are also qualities that define the finest of human
behavior—what it means not just to "be a man" but to be an *adult:*
to be peaceful but to be ready, to respect women, to be loyal to
friends and family, to be willing and able to change your mind, to
master yourself, to mentor the young, and to face the end with
dignity. There's also a darker side to this cultural legacy that continues to haunt us. In a 2015 *New York Times* article about disadvantaged boys in a low-income neighborhood of Portland, Oregon,
Jeff Knoblich, a school counselor for the Astor School, said, "Boys
get a message from a very young age to be a man, and to be a
man means you're strong and you don't cry and you don't show
your emotions. . . . I see boys suffering because of that, and a lot
of that comes out in aggressive behaviors." And in "The Darkest
Side of John Wayne," novelist and critic Jonathan Lethem asks,
"What other American icon comes so overloaded with reflections
of our national disasters of racism, sexual repression, violence
and authority? Who else thrusts the difficult question of what it
means to be a man in America so forcefully in our faces, daring
us to meet his gaze?" Though Lethem begins by calling Wayne,
with his "brute Republicanism," a "laughable political ignoramus,"
he quickly asserts that "John Wayne's resonance cuts across the
accidents of war and politics," and he concludes, "Wayne is finally
something other than either a man or a film star, but rather a kind
of archetypal figure."

The Western hero has remained an icon of masculinity, even if it belongs more to nostalgia than to current representations. But where did it begin? When did the Western cease being an afternoon matinee shoot-'em-up for mostly young boys and become a vehicle for mature themes, a retelling and a celebration of America's expansionist history, and a paradigm for becoming a certain kind of grown-up American male? And when and why did the Western begin to disappear from the cultural landscape? These are the essential questions that the story of John Wayne and John Ford's complicated, poignant, and iconic friendship can begin to answer.

*

Women may be less likely to seek out hero figures on whom they will model their identity and base their self-worth, but that paradigm fascinates me, both in art and in life. It's fortunate, then, though not coincidental, that this pattern lies at the heart of both John Ford's and John Wayne's personal stories. Both men began as seekers, modeling their lives on the examples of older, more experienced men, and both men ended, in their own realms, as celebrated icons—heroes to their fans and to much of America. But both men—John Ford especially—were flawed heroes, and both paid a price in their private lives.

No other director and actor created the ideal of the American hero more than Ford and Wayne, an ideal that evolved in seven major Westerns they made together. John Wayne's *The Alamo*—which he produced, starred in, and directed—and three late films Wayne made with other directors—Henry Hathaway's *True Grit*, Mark Rydell's *The Cowboys*, and Don Siegel's *The Shootist*—helped to deepen, and even rescue, Wayne's persona, which had begun to devolve into self-parody. Examining these films, and a handful of movies John Wayne appeared in made by other directors, such as *The Big Trail* and *Red River*, will help us discern what two of Hollywood's most influential and iconic figures had to say about what it meant to be a certain kind of American man.

Part One

THE
RELUCTANT
HERO

1

Birth of the Western Hero

Nobody should come to the movies unless he believes in heroes.
—JOHN WAYNE

When I pass on, I want to be remembered as
a guy who made Westerns.
—JOHN FORD

John Wayne as a symbol of America's strength at the height of the American century—from World War II throughout the Cold War era—was honed and brought to perfection by the great, irascible John Ford. Even if Ford did not become an archetypal figure himself, which he would have loathed, he is one of the most revered filmmakers in the history of American cinema. Martin Scorsese once said that Ford was "the essence of classical American cinema, and any serious person making films today, whether they know it or not, is affected by Ford."

John Ford's Westerns are compelling and beautiful. Brought up on silent movies, where visual images and music evoked emotions and told the story, John Ford carried his keen visual eye and love of indigenous music into talking pictures. "I had an eye for composition; that's all I had," he once said modestly, in one of his few serious comments about filmmaking. Film critic Lem Kitaj observed that "Ford's movies are visual ballads—they're sagas, they're poems. Just look at the film's titles," which often drew on army songs and traditional American ballads, such as "She Wore a Yellow Ribbon" and "My Darling Clementine." Ford's film composers transposed into their Western soundtracks traditional ballads and gospels, such as "Bury Me Not on the Lone Prairie," "Streets of Laredo," and "We Shall Gather at the River," underlying the sense of authenticity and often evoking a wistful melancholy. One could remove all the dialogue from many of Ford's Westerns and still follow the story and be moved by the images and the music alone.

As the documentarian Nick Redman observed, "He wasn't portraying America's *reality* but America's *mythology*," recognizing in the western expansion one of America's most enduring creation myths: how a unified nation stretched from sea to sea, bringing the dubious blessings of civilization to what it considered lawless territory. But he also explored much of America's actual experience: his Westerns are peopled with immigrants from many nations—the Irish, the Italians, the Swedes, the Chinese; his films both vilify Native Americans and pay homage to their bravery and to their tragic fate; in *Sergeant Rutledge* he dramatizes the perilous place of a black cavalryman wrongly accused of raping a white woman; and *The Searchers*, America's greatest Western and arguably one of the best films made in the twentieth century, recognizes the ugly fact of racial hatred woven into the American fabric, even in the heart of our most revered hero.

Artistry aside, the power of Ford's legacy owes no small part to the wide popularity of the Western genre. As feminist critic Jane Tompkins has noted, "From roughly 1900 to 1975 a significant portion of the adolescent male population spent every Saturday afternoon at the movies. What they saw there were Westerns. Roy Rogers, Tom Mix, Lash LaRue, Gene Autry, Hopalong Cassidy."

Saturday serials gave way to more sophisticated, grown-up Westerns in theaters—in no small part due to Ford's influence—

such as *High Noon* and *Shane* in the 1950s, but it was television in the mid-1950s and the 1960s where the Western truly flourished, with twenty-six Westerns running on prime-time television in the peak year of 1959. *Gunsmoke*—the longest-running Western in television history—and *The Life and Legend of Wyatt Earp* ushered in Westerns for grown-up audiences in 1955, and the genre flourished with high-quality Westerns after that: shows such as *Maverick*, introducing James Garner; *The Rifleman*, with an über-masculine Chuck Connors; *Wanted: Dead or Alive*, with a young Steve McQueen making a charismatic television series debut; *Laramie; Have Gun, Will Travel*, with another über-masculine star, Richard Boone; *Bonanza*, featuring an all-male household; *The Virginian; Wagon Train*, showcasing Ward Bond, briefly; *The Big Valley*, with Barbara Stanwyck; and Warner Bros.' *Sugarfoot, Bronco*, and *Cheyenne*. *Rawhide*—which introduced Clint Eastwood to the world—ran from 1959 to 1965. After 1969, no new TV Westerns were introduced to the public. *Death Valley Days*, narrated by Ronald Reagan before his political career, and *Gunsmoke* both ended in 1970. In the 1950s, thirty-one studio-made pictures were Westerns; by the 1990s, that number had dwindled to seven.

THE RISE OF THE AMERICAN WESTERN

Why was the Western such a powerful mode of storytelling throughout the second half of the last century? Tompkins has argued that the genre was a reaction to the nineteenth-century novel with its details of domesticity and feminine heroes, as well as an escape from encroaching civilization and feminine influences, in the form of the suffragette movement, temperance, and public decency leagues. Ford's *Stagecoach*, for example, opens with a gaggle of pinched, elderly, respectable townswomen running the beautiful prostitute, Dallas, out of town. In short, the wide-open spaces of the American West offered the idea of freedom from the constraints and hypocrisies of industrial society and the interior spaces of the Victorian novel: churches, parlors, bedrooms, kitchens. "The desert light," Tompkins writes, "and the desert space, the creak of saddle leather and the sun beating down, the horses' energy and force—these things promise a translation of the self into something purer and more authentic, more intense, more real," far from, in the final line of dialogue in Ford's *Stagecoach*, "the [dubious] blessings of civilization."

So, setting itself in contrast to the realms of society, church, and civilized law, the Western offered masculine realms of experience and codes of behavior that required physical strength, courage, and endurance. The Western also sought to answer the questions, What is honor? What is justice? What is loyalty? The Western concerns itself with how men come to understand and harness their instinctual urges and their physical power and what the consequences are of not succeeding in that endeavor.

And simultaneous with this rejection of the domestic space, the very model of masculinity was changing. Writers on sex, gender, and sexuality such as Michael S. Kimmel define a historical shift from late eighteenth- and early nineteenth-century masculine identities, like the "Genteel Patriarch"—a Jeffersonian landowner, family man, and benign patriarch—and the "Heroic Artisan"—economically self-sustaining craftsmen-citizens who cherish the democracy of the town meeting, like Paul Revere—to the "Marketplace Man," which became the prevailing boilerplate for masculine behavior throughout the twentieth century.

The Marketplace Man defines his masculinity by accumulating wealth, power, and status and is more likely to be an absentee landlord and an absent father than his forebears; the ad executives in *Mad Men* are prime examples from a later period. He increasingly defines himself in homosocial—all-male—societies, where his sense of masculinity comes from pitting and measuring himself against other men. His masculinity requires proof, often taking the form of exclusion of the "other": women, nonwhite men, nonnative-born men, homosexual men. In other words, "men prove their manhood in the eyes of other men," or, as playwright David Mamet has noted, "What men need is men's approval."

Kimmel cites psychologist Robert Brannon's markers of manhood in the following summary, which men must acquire to earn the approval of other men:

> 1. " 'No Sissy Stuff!' One may never do anything that even suggests femininity.
> 2. " 'Be a Big Wheel.' Masculinity is measured by power, success, wealth, and status.
> 3. " 'Be a Sturdy Oak.' Proving you're a man depends on never showing your emotions at all. Boys don't cry.
> 4. " 'Give 'Em Hell.' Exude an aura of manly daring and aggression."

These qualities are often attributed to John Wayne. As film critic Carl Freedman has noted, "Many movie stars have been admired for many varieties of manliness; but no other has *defined* masculinity to the extent that John Wayne has." But he was not the first to embody these qualities; rather, he perfected a masculine form that stretched far back into the silent era and to Ford's earliest days as a filmmaker.

John Ford's 1924 silent picture *The Iron Horse* is an early chapter in the great director's depiction of western expansion, mythologizing the men who cleared and fought for the frontier, laying the tracks for the transcontinental railroad. Stock characters appear that would reappear in later films: buffoonish Irish drunks (presented sympathetically), corrupt businessmen, and ethnic characters representing America's melting pot, which Ford both celebrated and presented comically, with their distrust of "forriners" and "Eyetalians," despite their own immigrant status.

The Iron Horse is a thrilling tale, beautifully filmed and acted, which includes a wise, countrified Abraham Lincoln, played by Charles Edward Bull, a precursor of Henry Fonda's folksy but dignified Abe in *Young Mr. Lincoln*. He's the spiritual father of the movie, America's first great "reluctant hero," and a role model for Davey Brandon, played by George O'Brien, who doesn't go looking for a fight and in fact vows *not* to fight to please his fiancée, Miriam Marsh, played by Madge Bellamy. We feel his frustration as he strains against his civilizing vow, in conflict with his need to avenge his father's murder, until, at the film's climax, O'Brien finally fights his archenemy, Deroux, a beefy villain played by Fred Kohler. Their lengthy battle begins in fisticuffs but ends in Greco-Roman wrestling as both men lose their shirts in the fight and are revealed in their half-naked masculinity. The camera admires them, especially a triumphant O'Brien leaning against a wall in *contrapposto* pose, shirtless, an image of masculine beauty. That arresting image signals that this is not just a typical adventure film, but one in which Ford manages to convey his celebration of the male form and psyche and his ability to present opposite points of view without resolving them or negating either side: to avoid violence is noble, but a fight can be a beautiful thing.

We also see Ford's double vision in his treatment of the Indians in the movie, whom the railway workers must hold off to complete their task. Throughout his movies, and especially in the later films such as *The Searchers* and *Cheyenne Autumn*, Ford revealed conflicting views of Native Americans: brave, yet not "civilized"; brutal, but not without honor. In *The Iron Horse*, Ford humanizes the warring Indians with a powerful yet intimate image: a dog lays its head on the body of a slain Indian brave (just as one of the buffoonish Irish drunks is redeemed by a heroic death and is tenderly embraced by his countrymen).

Davey Brandon and Abraham Lincoln can be seen as figures in a long continuum of reluctant heroes stretching from Harry Carey, "the good bad man," in the many silent Westerns Ford made with the veteran cowboy hero, to Henry Fonda's reluctant hero Wyatt Earp (who doesn't want to be the town sheriff) in *My Darling Clementine*, to John Wayne, who begins the major part of his

✳

Henry Fonda as the "jackanapes lawyer" in 1939's
Young Mr. Lincoln. Lincoln was one of Ford's heroes
and a model for the ideal man—folksy, humble, smart,
honorable, and willing to do what it takes.

career as the "good bad man" in *Stagecoach*. As Ford knew, "real men" don't seek fights, but when they must engage, they do.

In his search to tell the quintessential American story, Ford worked with many impressive leading actors, including Harry Carey, George O'Brien, Henry Fonda, and James Stewart, but in John Wayne he found his perfect hero, and the two men succeeded in defining an ideal of American masculinity that dominated for nearly half a century. Over the course of the twenty-three movies Ford and Wayne made together, including early films in which Wayne cropped up as an extra and a stuntman and a late-career documentary he narrated for Ford, Wayne's persona evolved from a charismatic "good bad man" in *Stagecoach* and *3 Godfathers*; to a U.S. Cavalry man devoted to his men but with no stomach for war in *Fort Apache* and *She Wore a Yellow Ribbon*; to a racist avenger in *The Searchers*; to an over-the-hill hero whose exploits are appropriated by the new man of the conquered frontier in *The Man Who Shot Liberty Valance*, Ford's last great Western and arguably his last great film.

MEN AS MENTORS

The Western is often about handing down a code of behavior, in which an older, sometimes over-the-hill father figure instructs a youth—preferably but not always a son—in the challenging ways of mastering himself. In John Wayne's Westerns, the conferring of masculinity on a youth is a sacred duty. As he matured and became less powerful as an action hero, he was especially good in this role, particularly in *The Cowboys*, *True Grit*, and *The Shootist*. From the mentee's perspective, living up to a father figure's expectations lies at the very heart of the matter, and to disappoint the father, or fail to be recognized by him, is devastating. Once a boy becomes a man, he must teach other boys to undertake the journey. So, the Western hero is sometimes a youth in search of a father figure or a father in search of a son, or a man out to avenge a wronged father or redeem a shamed one. Or a tough old coot who has no sons to grace with his recognition, so he must teach the offspring of strangers.

In seven Westerns that Ford made with John Wayne, his definition of manhood is much more nuanced, humane, non-exclusionary, and achievable than the stereotypical John Wayne image. To summarize, in Ford's world, to "be a man," one must possess the following traits:

1. Humility, courtesy, and the keeping of one's word, as the Ringo Kid does in *Stagecoach*. Bullies and warmongers need not apply.
2. The toughness to endure while protecting the weak, coupled with respect—even awe!—for women, like Bob Hightower in *3 Godfathers*.
3. The ability to speak truth to power, regardless of the consequences, as Captain Kirby York does in *Fort Apache*.
4. Loyalty to comrades, against all odds, like Captain Nathan Brittles in *She Wore a Yellow Ribbon*.
5. The ability to admit one is wrong and to change one's mind, like Lieutenant Colonel Kirby Yorke in *Rio Grande* and Ethan Edwards in *The Searchers*.
6. Fidelity to oneself in changing times, without expectation of recognition or reward, like Tom Doniphon in *The Man Who Shot Liberty Valance*.

Indeed, many of Ford's heroes fail in their intended tasks, but what is important is their willingness to do the right thing—to *engage*. Despite failure, they remain heroes because of the effort put forward. It's being *willing*, as John Wayne's character, John Bernard Books, says in *The Shootist*.

Though John Wayne indelibly embodied the Fordian hero, when he turned to producing his own pictures—*Big Jim McLain*, *The Alamo*, *The Green Berets*—the results were often derailed by his ultra-patriotism. Unlike Ford, he ended up making propaganda, not art. Yet at the end of his career as an actor in the post-Fordian movies *True Grit*, *The Cowboys*, and *The Shootist*, his persona finally evolved in satisfying ways, illustrating three additional masculine virtues:

· the willingness to pass on one's knowledge to a younger generation
· the ability to laugh at oneself and make fun of one's image
· the ability to know the end when it comes and accept it with dignity

These last films rescued John Wayne from ending his long career as a caricature of himself, giving a more realistic humanity to his iconic image.

*

Much of Wayne's legendary status rests on his roles as a man of action, a loner, a hardened soul willing to use violence to get the job done, if necessary, and more intent on proving himself in the eyes of his comrades—whether cowboys or cavalrymen or soldiers of World War II—than wooing women. This raises the question, why does "a man's man" prefer the company of men and shun women?

The controversial writer and polemicist Jack Donovan has made his lifework an examination, and a celebration, of traditional, undiluted masculinity. In *The Way of Men*, he notes that "when men compete against each other for status, they are competing for *each other's* approval. The women whom men find most desirable have historically been attracted to—or been claimed by—men who were feared or revered by other men." The operative word here is "historically," because this paradigm has clearly shifted in the last decades as women looked less for a protector and more for an equal partner and as the popularity of rock stars and ethnic actors replaced the image of an idealized, white, and larger-than-life iconic hero. But aspects of this heroic ideal are reflected again and again in Western films and in most of John Ford's oeuvre.

In the many Westerns and war pictures Wayne starred in, there is a marked absence of women. Men prove themselves in the eyes of other men, and that is their fundamental, existential challenge. A man of action instead of a romantic hero, Wayne seldom wooed the girl, and when he did, the relationship was often expressed through antagonism (*The Quiet Man, McLintock!*) or doomed to be sacrificed on the altar of duty and esprit de corps among men (*Rio Grande, They Were Expendable*). Strong women do appear in Ford's films (notably in *Rio Grande, The Quiet Man,* and *The Searchers*), but their actions are usually dependent on and secondary to the male hero's.

One reason for the relative lack of women characters is that the reinvention of the Western for grown-up audiences, credited to John Ford's *Stagecoach,* came on the heels of the "kiddie" Westerns churned out by Poverty Row studios such as Monogram and Republic, where John Wayne toiled for nine years, learning his craft but well aware of (and embarrassed by) the simplistic— and second-rate—quality of much of the final product. Because those Westerns were aimed mostly at young boys, the absence of a romantic story line suited their audience: no yucky love scenes, and few or no women. In these B Westerns, boys could escape from overprotective mothers and nagging schoolmarms into an all-male world of friendship and derring-do. And could those cowboys fight, and leap on a horse! So it's possible that the dearth of strong women characters in serious, grown-up Westerns stems, in part, from the genre's origin as children's entertainment, mostly for young boys, as well as a rejection of what was perceived as a feminized, overly restrictive society.

So when women appear at all, it's usually in the form of a sweetheart or a prairie wife who tries to keep the hero at home, away from the quest that calls out to him. Or as her opposite: the tough, sexually available saloon girl, who knows the score but is usually cast aside when the quest is fulfilled. In other words, the usual virgin-whore paradigm.

Ford, however, included in many of his movies another female archetype: the strong, tough, and loving matriarch, best represented in his story of Welsh coal miners, *How Green Was My Valley*, and in John Steinbeck's Depression-era tale, *The Grapes of Wrath*. His Catholic background might have been an influence here, with its reverence for the Virgin Mary, but he has also said that the mothers in those two movies were reminiscent of his own mother, and they are the moral centers of both films. In either case, he was able to attribute traditionally "male" values—courage, toughness, outspokenness—to many of his female characters (these qualities would find their apotheosis in the great, fiery Maureen O'Hara, arguably Ford's and Wayne's favorite actress).

THE FALL

Questioning traditional masculine images and behavior in popular culture gained traction in the late 1960s and the 1970s, when Westerns were disappearing as a dominant film and television genre. This shift coincided with the second wave of feminism, and in part that questioning—that searching for new models of masculinity—was also a response to America's disastrous military intervention in Vietnam, in which the wisdom of the elders and masculine virtues such as valor and loyalty were increasingly seen as fallible or wrongheaded. *M*A*S*H*, *Five Easy Pieces*, *Easy Rider*, *The Graduate*, *Catch-22*, *Cannonball Run*, and countless other popular books and movies satirized the American hero or called into question masculine virtues that had been taken for granted and had been nobly expressed in American cinema since its inception—especially in Westerns.

As post-Vietnam mistrust of the armed services grew, and an all-volunteer army relegated the military to mostly blue-collar American men, masculine models in popular culture increasingly appeared outside the realm of war pictures and Westerns. Rock music glorified the strutting, peacock male, introducing a some-times androgynous element to the masculine image and making it possible for masculine icons to be skinny, pallid, not convention-ally handsome: Keith Richards, Mick Jagger, Bob Dylan, David Bowie.

But what still lurked behind alternate, late twentieth-century representations of masculine objects of desire, especially in tran-scendent artists like Bob Dylan and the Band, were vestiges of the Western hero, in style and dress. Dylan still dresses like a Western dandy, and Mick Jagger, in one of his rare cinematic performances, played the nineteenth-century Australian outlaw Ned Kelly. Dylan, for that matter, wrote a haunting score for and appeared in *Pat Garrett and Billy the Kid*. Maybe it's the Western style of dress—most men look good in blue jeans, vests, neckerchiefs, boots, and hats!

Proper Westerns still appear from time to time on premium cable and on the big screen, occasionally enjoying critical and popular success, such as A&E's *Longmire* and HBO's iconoclastic *Deadwood* and a handful of Robert Duvall–, Clint Eastwood–, and Kevin Costner–helmed big-screen Westerns. There are also latter-day incarnations with incredible cultural power, like *Star Wars*. But the idea of what it means to be a man, and how a boy *becomes* a man, has shifted dramatically. As the Western disappears from the cultural landscape, what has replaced it as a paradigm of how boys become men?

One genre where we still see this drama played out is in African American films, such as those produced, directed, and written by John Singleton. In his seminal 1991 film, *Boyz n the Hood*, a stark contrast is made between a boy brought up with a father, who does the right thing, and those brought up without fathers, who become gangstas. As Furious Styles, played by Lau-rence Fishburne, tells his son Tre, played by Cuba Gooding Jr., "Any fool with a dick can make a baby, but only a real man can raise his children." Singleton's 2001 film, *Baby Boy*, also explores themes of masculinity in struggling black communities, where boys must become men in a world where there are few positive masculine role models.

But in many contemporary male-bonding "bromance" comedies—Seth Rogen and Judd Apatow's *Pineapple Express* and *The Hangover I, II,* and *III* or Vince Vaughn in *Wedding Crashers,* to name a few—the hero is celebrated as a man-child: clueless, self-indulgent, often charming but more often feckless and at the mercy of empowered and demanding women. Not only is the hero's extended adolescence presented to be enjoyed rather than outgrown, but there are few or no father figures present with the authority to help the hero grow up. Instead, the audience is asked to identify with, and to laugh at, heroes who find themselves comically baffled and overwhelmed by the complexities and contradictions of contemporary culture, but not to admire them. And contemporary action movies that celebrate the feats of masculine heroes are now mostly incarnations of comic book characters— the Superman, Batman, and Spider-Man franchises—in which the hero is a boy's fantasy version of mastery and triumph, aided by special effects, supernatural powers, comic villains, and gleeful suspension of disbelief. Not to say they aren't enormous fun, but they don't take seriously the mythic hero and his—and, at last, sometimes *her*—struggle to achieve a kind of maturity and grace.

At the same time we enjoy these boy-hero comedies and superpower fantasies, we still cling to the archetype of the Western loner, out clearing brush on his ranch in cowboy hat and boots, an image put to use by Ronald Reagan and George W. Bush. They managed to project their inner Marlboro Man—who resembled *Gunsmoke*'s Matt Dillon as played by James Arness—cementing their popularity, mostly with conservative white males, whether or not they truly embodied that status. The Republican Party generally has long sought to cast itself as the party of Western masculinity, regardless of where in the country particular candidates hail from; note that Donald Trump made a pilgrimage to the John

Wayne Museum in Winterset, Iowa—Wayne's birthplace—and got one of Wayne's daughters, Aissa, to endorse his candidacy, not to mention the adolescent bragging about, well, "size" in one of the Republican Party debates. Is this simply nostalgia or a deeper yearning for something that's been lost in the last decades of the twentieth century?

That sense of loss already seemed to cling to the later Ford-Wayne Westerns. In *The Man Who Shot Liberty Valance*, the heroic gunfighter played by John Wayne has become a marginalized, outsider figure, replaced by Jimmy Stewart's prairie lawyer turned politician, who has grasped where real power increasingly lies. In *The Searchers*, their greatest film, Wayne plays the racist Ethan Edwards, who finally turns away from his lust for vengeance but nonetheless ends up an outcast from family and community, framed in a dark doorway against the vast emptiness of the western sky.

Perhaps that sense of longing, that nostalgia, has to do with not only a romanticized and vanished era of American history but a certain kind of male who once dominated American culture but now seems on the embattled fringe: those men who seem hardwired to protect women, children, and country. When their protection is taken for granted or no longer needed, or when their efforts fail to keep loved ones from harm, that heroic urge becomes dangerously thwarted.

Would-be protectors can turn into vengeful predators; we see that in *The Searchers*. Ford knew that, and he sought to keep in balance tenderer emotions that bind together communities—families, villages, military compounds—with the camaraderie among men devoted to patrolling the perimeters. Sometimes the fight to protect ends up destroying the very thing it set out to preserve in the first place.

2

The Good Bad Man

Dammit. The son of a bitch looked like a man.
—RAOUL WALSH ON JOHN WAYNE

To live outside the law you must be honest.
—BOB DYLAN

THE BIG BREAK

Director John Ford—born John Martin Feeney and known as Sean O'Fearna (in the Gaelic), Pappy, Coach, or Jack Ford—elevated John Wayne from property boy, bit actor, and occasional stuntman to leading man in his classic 1939 film *Stagecoach*, launching the strapping actor on a career that would eventually make him the number one movie star in the world. But it wasn't Ford who gave John "Duke" Wayne his first starring role in pictures. It was Raoul Walsh, in a Western epic released in 1930 called *The Big Trail*. Wayne was well suited to play the new Adam, a frontiersman confronting an untamed, unspoiled wilderness with courage and optimism. He wore his essential goodness on his sleeve, and the characters around him often sought to exploit it. More significantly, the audience responded to it. In *The Big Trail*, he didn't need to wear the signature white hat, a staple of the early Hollywood Western for children, to show he was the good guy. His innocence, his courage, his resolve, his loyalty to a slain friend, and his tenderness to a feisty young woman on the wagon train he is guiding through the wilderness immediately signal a hero to root for. The fact that he has to be persuaded to take on the task also helps define him: the true hero is a *reluctant* hero.

That "remarkable quality of innocence," as film director and film historian Peter Bogdanovich has noted, defined John Wayne right from the start and immediately made him a charismatic, and sympathetic, presence on-screen despite his lack of theatrical experience and film technique. His performance got Ford's attention and made him think that the handsome, well-mannered, oversized, somewhat shy property boy—good mostly for moving scenery and occasional stunt work—might turn out to be an actor after all. But it would take another nine years before Ford gave John Wayne a chance by casting him as the Ringo Kid in *Stagecoach*. When later asked why he waited so long before offering Wayne a leading role, Ford said that he had kept his eye on Duke all along but had waited because he felt that "Duke wasn't ready. He had to develop his skills as an actor. . . . I wanted some pain written on his face to offset the innocence."

✳

Marion Morrison's football coach at USC, Howard Jones, had gotten several of his athletes summer jobs moving scenery and props at Fox and, later, working as extras in John Ford's *Salute*, about an Army-Navy football game at Annapolis. Morrison rounded up his fellow football players, including his future friend and sometime rival Ward Bond, who would become a memorable character actor and a reliable member of the John Ford stock company, as well as a longtime friend of both Ford's and Wayne's. But Ford first met Duke Morrison when Duke showed up to work on the Fox Studios lot in the summer of 1928, herding a flock of geese on the set of Ford's silent picture *Mother Machree*, a sentimental paean to Irish immigrants. The director was a tall, pipe-smoking, redheaded, heavy-featured man in spectacles who was surprisingly graceful on his feet. At thirty-three years of age, he would win his first Best Director Academy Award in 1936 for *The Informer*, a haunting, shadows-and-fog drama about a hapless man, played by the larger-than-life, barrel-chested Victor McLaglen, who informs against his friend in the Irish Republican Army. Ford had directed over sixty silent films by the time he met Duke—learning everything he could from, and finally surpassing, his mentors: his older brother Frank Ford and the silent Western star Harry Carey—and he had established a reputation as a crusty, quick-tempered Irishman inspiring fear and adoration in equal measure. Six feet tall and a former high school football player himself, Ford was not a man to be crossed. He took one look at the even larger—six-foot-four, two-hundred-pound—callow youth who stood off camera shyly corralling his flock of geese and instantly sized him up.

In romantic comedies, the hero and heroine "meet cute" and usually start out as adversaries. In male-bonding movies, the two buddies usually begin with a fight, testing each other's mettle, before becoming friends. So it happened with Ford and Wayne. Upon learning that Wayne was a USC football player, Ford tackled him to the ground. But Wayne got up and repositioned himself, taking Ford crashing down to the ground in one sudden move. The entire crew held its breath, waiting for the explosion of wrath. Surprisingly, it didn't come. Instead, Ford got up and calmly walked away. Duke—still Marion Morrison—had made an impression. Ford ended up casting Duke as an uncredited extra in *Mother Machree* and as an uncredited officer in another 1928 silent film, *Four Sons*, before returning him to the status of third assistant property man.

Years later, Ford recalled,

I met Duke—he was very bright and energetic and I realized at the time he was hooked on movies. . . . I got him a job as third assistant prop man . . . [he's] the man who does the manual labor. And he was good; I remember one incident. I was doing a picture called *Four Sons* and there's a scene where a woman receives word about her son, it's a very dramatic scene. She's sitting alone in this room; in the back there's a big open door. We tried a couple of times, the third time she was great. In the back[ground] there's this big gangling Wayne sweeping the leaves off the floor; halfway through he looked in, gave a gasp of horror, dropped his broom and started running for the gate. . . . I said, that's a natural mistake, I know you're new to the business. Forget it! We'll do the scene again and it'll be better. He was very chagrined.

Duke recalled, however, that he was dragged back to Ford, who "bent me over and kicked me in the ass." Despite being embarrassed by his experiences on *Four Sons* and *Mother Machree*, Wayne developed a keen admiration of the director that would last his entire life. He recalled, "I had no ambition to be an actor, I had no desire for it." What he wanted was "to be like Jack Ford! My whole set up was that he was my mentor and my ideal! I think that deep down inside, he's one of the greatest human beings that I have ever known. And I've known quite a few people in my life. And as a consequence I took more interest in the business."

By that time, his interest in pursuing a law career, his course of study at USC, had waned considerably. Wayne recalled that just being around Pappy Ford made him think seriously about his future:

When I went back to school that year, I looked around, and the kids that I knew who were going to take Law around the time that I would be taking it, I'd see one, and I'd think, well his father has a law firm, another one, his uncle has one . . . and whether or not I'm brighter, I'll end up writing their briefs for them! I'll be in the back room for ten years before I can even get started in the business, or else I'll have to hang up a shingle and take the kind of legal work I wouldn't be interested in. So for this reason, it really started preying on me.

It was just as well, because an injury derailed his football career and scholarship, and neither he nor his struggling family had the funds to cover his USC tuition.

Still not convinced that he wanted to be an actor, Duke realized he could make a contribution to Ford's movies beyond being a third assistant propman. He had the strength and athletic ability to do stunt work, and his opportunity came quickly on Ford's 1930 film *Men Without Women*, a tale of male camaraderie and danger that takes place entirely aboard a submarine, combining, incidentally, two of Ford's lifelong interests: the sea, and the fraternity of men living and working with other men, which would become a major theme in Ford's oeuvre. Duke Wayne recalled the challenge of doing stunt work on the picture:

> We were between San Diego and Catalina, and I was up on the midship deck, and I had on a blue sweater and a watch cap. We were using a mine sweeper for a camera ship. . . . It was a gray day, and [Ford] was shooting into backlight, and two destroyers went by belching that black smoke, and it was just a beautiful scene. . . . There were big swells and steely gray water. . . . It was scary looking water. . . . [T]he navy boat is a big boat and they don't handle quite as easy.

Ford had reportedly promised Duke $75 for every dangerous stunt he performed, such as diving into those steely gray waters off Catalina, which he did repeatedly. But Ford never made good his offer; instead of the $450 he expected in addition to his salary of $35 per week, Duke was only given an additional $7.50 for risking his life. Duke later said, "I should have complained . . . [but] I was still a shy, timid person, always embarrassed about speaking up for my rights." So any ambitions Wayne had for acting took second place behind his stunt work, until *The Big Trail* that same year.

✳

Like John Ford, the director Raoul Walsh was the son of Irish immigrants from back east whose fifty-year career in Hollywood began as an actor and assistant director in silent films. His acting career ended after a freak road accident when a jackrabbit crashed into his windshield on location in Arizona, taking out his left eye. When the doctors offered him a glass eye, he turned it down, grousing that he'd just lose it in a poker game, and opted for a rakish black eye patch instead. Ford, plagued by weak eyesight, also adopted a black eye patch later in life—possibly in imitation of Walsh—which might have then influenced John Wayne's Academy Award–winning role as Rooster Cogburn in Henry Hathaway's *True Grit*. (Charles Portis's brilliant, comedic novel simply describes Cogburn as having an empty eye socket, unadorned by any eye patch, black or otherwise, suggesting that the touch was an homage of Wayne's devising.)

The disfigurement ruled Walsh out of appearing in pictures but focused his mind on directing them. Also like Ford, Walsh was tough, prolific, and brilliant, directing sixty films including the classics *The Big Trail, High Sierra*, and *White Heat*. In 1929, Walsh set out to find a lead actor to replace studio favorite Gary Cooper, who wasn't available for his ambitious, wide-screen Western epic, *The Big Trail*. He happened to notice a strapping, fresh-faced, good-looking young man moving props at Fox Studios. He was struck by the youth's broad frame and the ease with which he carried an overstuffed chair hoisted lightly over one shoulder.

By the time Raoul Walsh laid eyes on Duke Morrison, the only on-screen experience Morrison had was as a bit player and stuntman in a handful of Ford's movies; his real value to the Ford Stock Company was still his brawn behind the scenes. When Walsh saw

✳

Marion Morrison: a callow youth in Raoul Walsh's
The Big Trail in 1930. Two years passed before John Ford forgave
Duke Wayne for working with another director.

Morrison easily hoisting that chair above his head, he grasped the young man's potential, giving him a lead role in *The Big Trail* as Breck Coleman, a trapper out to avenge the murder of a friend who becomes a scout for a wagon train heading west on what would become the Oregon Trail. Walsh later recalled, "He had a good height. He was bare breasted. It was a hot day. He wasn't wearing a shirt. He was a good looking boy. . . . He had a certain western hang to his shoulders. . . . [A] certain way of holding yourself and walking is typical of a real westerner and he had it." His youth and relative inexperience suited him well for the role of the reluctant hero who agrees to undertake the quest on behalf of his murdered friend, instead of seeking glory for himself.

It was Walsh, not Ford, who changed Marion Morrison's name to John Wayne, inspired in part by Revolutionary War hero "Mad" Anthony Wayne, though Duke apparently took the name "John" out of deference to John Ford, whom he hero-worshipped from the start. Many years later, when Ford's grandson, Dan Ford, asked him if Wayne borrowed the name from him, Ford answered, "Yeah. He wanted a name sort of similar to mine. Which is flattering."

Because John Wayne reached his greatest fame as a mature, hardened, barrel-chested man with thinning hair, it's rather amazing to see him as the lithe, cheerful, and boyishly handsome twenty-three-year-old Breck Coleman in Walsh's epic. Dressed in buckskins and wearing moccasins, he embodies America's "natural man," like Natty Bumppo in *The Last of the Mohicans*, or Huck Finn rafting down the Mississippi with the runaway slave, Jim, or Davy Crockett in his iconic raccoon-tailed hat. Taught by Indians how to survive in the wilderness, Coleman even delivers a poetic soliloquy about the deep pleasures of sleeping in the open air under a radiant moon. He undertakes the arduous and dangerous journey not out of a need to prove himself or to seek glory but because he *has* to.

In his first major role, John Wayne played opposite a cast of seasoned stage actors, including Tyrone Power Sr., the beautiful Marguerite Churchill, and Ian Keith. Though he lacks technique and training, his naturalness on-screen outshines his fellow actors; the gracefulness of his large frame is already apparent, as are his effortless strength and, when called upon, a fierce resolve in his eyes. Yet he's also a sweet and playful lover; in an early scene, in one swift motion he lifts a would-be sweetheart off a piano bench, twirls her in the air, and catches her in his arms, planting a playful kiss on her lips. His grace and economy of motion—his sheer joy of movement—are a pleasure to watch. And because *The Big Trail* is a sweeping saga of America's western migration, filmed on location in stunning landscapes, John Wayne's persona as a great American hero—indeed, an embodiment of America itself—begins with Raoul Walsh's magnificent film.

Too bad it failed at the box office.

Fox's expensive investment in Grandeur CinemaScope techniques, which required refitting theaters with special equipment, and its steep production costs including two thousand extras, location shoots in four states, and a legion of horses, oxen, and Conestoga wagons, came close to bankrupting the studio. *The Big Trail* was the *Cleopatra*, the *Heaven's Gate*, of its day—a financial disaster wreaked by the weight of its own ambition. After a memorable debut in a leading role, the newly christened John Wayne—still known to his friends by his childhood nickname Duke—failed to have his contract picked up by Fox, and he was relegated to appearing in B Westerns for Poverty Row studios like Mascot, Monogram, and Republic, mechanically churned out for the "kiddie trade." He'd hoped that his former mentor, John Ford, might use him in a real movie for grown-ups, but that, so far, was not to be.

Ford didn't yet consider him leading role material. "I like[d] Duke's style from the very first time I met him," he later said. "I could see that here was a boy who was working for something— not like most of the other guys, just hanging around to pick up a few fast bucks. Duke was really ambitious and willing to work." So Ford wasn't happy when Walsh poached Duke right from under his nose, and he was put out with Wayne for having defected, even if it meant a lead role in a major film. Ford considered it an act of betrayal. He had wanted to bring Wayne along slowly, and he felt the young man wasn't ready. So he refused to even speak to the hopeful actor for two years, though Duke tried to re-ingratiate himself. While he didn't blame Ford's cold shoulder on his appearing in *The Big Trail*, he did recall,

> I remember he was evidently mad at me at one time . . . when I first started with him as an actor, and I quit working in production, and I said hello to him one morning and he didn't answer me, and I thought, well, he had something else on his mind. Next day I said, "hi, Coach," and it looked like a deliberate pass. Third day I got right in front of him and I said, "Pappy, hello." And he didn't speak to me! So, I didn't bother him again, for two years.

Nor did he appear in any other major film after *The Big Trail* for nearly a decade. His next film was *Girls Demand Excitement* for Fox in 1931, in which he played a college basketball player, again opposite Marguerite Churchill but in a cheaply produced film he knew was terrible. Even his old friends at USC razzed him about it when the film was released. He then played an architect in *Three Girls Lost*, also for Fox that same year, opposite Loretta Young. Duke had dated the actress's younger sister Polly Ann in his first year at USC, so he knew Loretta and enjoyed working with her. But these performances were underwhelming, and the good reviews for his work in *The Big Trail* faded.

IN THE WILDERNESS

Duke had a strong work ethic and a genuine desire to excel—he hated what he considered his own mediocrity and worked mightily to transcend it—so he was nearly despondent at the apparent end of his burgeoning career in pictures. Pappy Ford was ignoring him, too, so there was no going back to that promising start.

Harry Cohn at Columbia Pictures, then a well-thought-of but smaller studio, was impressed enough with Duke to hire him to star in low-budget Westerns and action films that were "calculated to appeal to rural and small-town audiences." Duke starred in Columbia's *Arizona* in 1931, but things went badly for him at the studio when Cohn accused him of having an affair with a young actress he had his own sights on. "Keep your goddamn fly buttoned at my studio," he barked at his young actor, humiliating him. Duke was further humiliated when Cohn next cast him to play the corpse in a low-budget thriller titled *The Deceiver*. It was a huge comedown. A fainter heart would have quit at that point, but Duke soldiered on. For six months he accepted Cohn's punishment by appearing as a second-string actor in a series of low-budget oaters—horse operas—such as *Maker of Men, Texas Cyclone*, and *Two-Fisted Law*. It seemed his fate was set.

Perhaps the example of John Ford, the first true artist Wayne recognized in his life, kept him going, despite their freeze-out. And there was also his intention to marry his college sweetheart, a socially prominent, Hispanic American Catholic named Josephine Saenz, whose family didn't quite approve of young Duke Wayne, who seemed to be squandering his youth playing corpses and oafish cowboys in the still rather quasi-respectable motion picture business. Had he stayed with his plans to become a lawyer, it would have made him more acceptable to Josephine's status-conscious family.

Josephine was a haughty beauty, a devoted Catholic, whose Hispanic background made her all the more exotic and appealing to Duke. She had everything Duke's childhood had lacked: social status, money, security, even glamour. From the age of seven, Duke had grown up on a hardscrabble farm in arid, rattlesnake-infested Antelope valley, north of Los Angeles, after his father, Clyde Morrison, had failed to make a decent living as a pharmacist's clerk back in Winterset, Iowa. Duke's engagement to Josephine dragged on, despite her parents' misgivings, until he could find some measure of success and begin making money. He was floundering, but he was hardworking, smart, and ambitious.

In 1932, Columbia Pictures, like Fox Studios before it, declined to pick up his option, and Duke was unemployed. Not only did Cohn drop Wayne, but he circulated rumors that he was "a drunk and a rebel." Duke thought about giving up. "For a year I couldn't get work," he recalled, "and I was thinking of going into the fight racket, which I was too old for." So when he was finally offered a role in one of the B Westerns churned out by Mascot Pictures, a Poverty Row studio run by the shrewd, cigar-chomping producer Nat Levine, he took the job. The money was terrible—roughly half his previous salary at Columbia Pictures—and the serials and action films were second-rate, strictly for the kids. This was his lot for the next nine years, his youthful beauty seemingly squandered, but the period would become a valuable apprenticeship as much as a purgatory. He was making a steady if modest living, and he was discovering—despite the grueling, physical toll it took on him— that he loved making movies.

✳

Duke secured the lead in three twelve-episode serials, beginning with 1932's *Shadow of the Eagle*, a hackneyed story about a carnival stunt flier filmed, of all places, in Antelope valley, the same barren landscape Duke had hated as a boy. It was a grueling experience, working eighteen-hour days in the pitiless sun, but there was a major reward: Duke worked alongside the extraordinary stuntman Yakima "Yak" Canutt, who became a close friend and teacher. Yak doubled Duke Wayne in the difficult stunts, and because each of the twelve episodes ended on a cliff-hanger, there were many. Wayne biographer Ronald L. Davis described their bonding:

> Most of the company decided to spend the night on location rather than drive back to Los Angeles for only a few

hours' sleep. Some of the crew built a fire, and Wayne sat down in front of it and pulled out a bottle of whiskey. Canutt sauntered over and knelt down beside him. Without saying anything, Duke handed Yak the bottle, and the stuntman uncorked it and took a long swig. Form that moment on, they were lifelong friends as well as professional colleagues. "Wayne," the stuntman declared, "[was] a regular kind of guy."

With Canutt as his guide, Wayne mastered stunts such as the "crupper mount"—leaping up over the rear of a horse from a running start—and staged innovative fistfights. The two men discovered that a real fight looks staged from the camera's vantage point but a staged fight looks real; their realistic but safe way to choreograph a fight changed the way such scenes were staged from there on out. Canutt later remarked, "Wayne got to be terrific. I used to think he'd put up a better picture fight than most of the stuntmen." He was also learning the nuts and bolts of lighting and camera angles, and even took a turn as a "singing cowboy," playing Singin' Sandy Saunders in *Riders of Destiny* (1933) for Monogram. But the voice was dubbed in by a baritone actor while Wayne mouthed the words, making him feel like "a goddamn pansy."

Another innovation of Duke's was to make the cowboy-hero more realistic, in an era when the good guy wore white, strummed a guitar, and didn't drink or smoke; after all, the low-budget serials had to pass muster with kids' parents. But Wayne had always revered the silent screen cowboy Harry Carey, who made twenty-six movies with John Ford in the 1920s and who taught young Ford much of what he knew about making movies.

Although he was well educated and came from a distinguished family back east, Carey was craggy, rough-hewn, with dirt on his clothes and a scowl on his face. With Ford, he perfected the role of the "good bad man" as the outlaw Cheyenne Harry in twenty-three Westerns, beginning in 1917 and appearing in Ford's first feature-length movie, *Straight Shooting*, also in 1917. Wayne would later say that Carey "projected a quality that we like to think of in men of the West. Ford and the great Western directors built on his authenticity."

As a lad in Glendale, Duke had loved Harry Carey's movies, along with other Western stars like Hoot Gibson and William S. Hart, but Carey was his favorite. "I made up my mind I was going to play a real man to the best of my ability," Wayne later said. "I knocked the stuffing out of the goody-goody Boy Scout cowboy hero and made him a believable guy. My dad told me that if I got into a fight, to win it." In an attempt to distance himself from the singing cowboy of B Western pictures, he took Harry Carey as one of his models.

> When I started, I knew I was no actor, and I went to work on this Wayne thing. It was as deliberate and studied a projection as you'll ever see. I figured I needed a gimmick, so I dreamed up the drawl, the squint, and a way of moving meant to suggest that I wasn't looking for trouble but would just as soon throw a bottle at your head as not. It was a hit-or-miss project for a while, but it began to develop. . . . I even had to practice saying *ain't*.

PAPPY FORD

While Duke was growing up watching Harry Carey on the big screen, young John Ford was learning the ropes of the movie business.

"Pappy was full of bullshit, but it was a delightful sort of bullshit," Henry Fonda once said about John Ford, with whom he made nine films. "He likes to claim that he was just a lace-curtain Irishman from the State of Maine who had come out here to do stunts for his brother, and they had made him a director because he could yell loud."

Ford rarely gave straight answers to questions about himself, especially about his personal life, because he projected an identity

✳

1938 portrait of John Ford: brilliant, sensitive,
artistic—and a merciless taskmaster.

of his own creation; to him, the facts of the past were useful only as the seeds of myth. "The truth about my life is nobody's damn business but my own," he growled to his interlocutors. Woe to any journalist or would-be apprentice who showed up on a John Ford set hoping for an in-depth interview. As film scholar Lem Kitaj comments in Nick Redman's documentary *Becoming John Ford*, "Ford's famous act was to pretend to know nothing, when he actually knew everything; he pretended not to care when he actually cared very much . . . he was this cantankerous, grumpy guy who wouldn't engage."

Ford was born John Martin Feeney, the youngest of thirteen children, seven of whom died in infancy. For fourteen years, the Feeneys lived over a saloon on Center Street in Portland, Maine, before moving to a rambling farmhouse on a two-hundred-acre farm on Cape Elizabeth, where John—called Jack by his family— was born on February 1, 1894. Feeney ran his farm but also managed a saloon in the nearby town of Two Lights. What Ford remembered from those early years was a happy childhood in proximity to the sea, engendering a lifelong love of maritime adventures. In 1897, Feeney moved his large family—his wife and his six surviving children, Patrick, Mary, Frank, Edward, Josephine, and John—back to Portland, this time to Danforth Street. There, he opened a bar and restaurant in Gorham's Corner, a somewhat seedy neighborhood near the waterfront. The saloons were the heart of the city for hardworking Irish immigrants, and in Gorham's Corner, Saturday night brawls and rivalries between ancient clans often broke out among men escaping the harshness of their lives in the new country. Raised in a rowdy household with three older brothers and a tempestuous saloon-keeping father, Ford would later seek to re-create the sense of male camaraderie, fueled by liquor, he'd grown up with.

In the years before Prohibition, Feeney's saloon prospered (though his wife and oldest son, Patrick, were disapproving teetotalers), and the family moved to the more respectable Monument Street and then to a triplex on Sheridan Street that they shared with two other Irish families, the Mahoneys and the Meyers. They had finally arrived as "lace-curtain Irish," though Ford's sympathies would always be with "the shanty Irish." As a director, he would be drawn, again and again, to sagas of the struggling poor, sometimes presenting the buffoonery of hard-drinking men but ultimately insisting on their dignity, notably in *The Grapes of Wrath* and *How Green Was My Valley*, with the Welsh standing in for the Irish. "I am of the proletariat. My people were peasants," Ford once said, tersely, with subdued pride. "They came here, were educated, and served this country well."

Producer and actor Charles FitzSimons, brother of the Irish actress Maureen O'Hara, believed that John Ford's "one great emotional tragedy" in his life was that

> he hadn't been born in Ireland. He wanted to be as Irish as anybody could be, so he wore an Irish tweed jacket with the collar turned up. . . . If he wore a hat, it would have the brim turned down all around, and he would often tie his slacks up around his ankles. The reason for that was that he was try-ing to be a native Irishman. In Ireland the grass is long and wet, and we will very often tie up the legs of our pants to save them from getting wet. Of course we wear Irish tweed jackets and always wear the brim of our hat down and the collar of our coat up, so the rain runs off. . . . Ford didn't really know that, but he was adopting what he thought was native Irish garb. He was a deliberately self-directed charac-ter, determined to make himself a native Irishman.

Ford pays tribute to the Irish in film after film, from *The Iron Horse* to *The Informer*, which won him his first Best Director Acad-emy Award, and most famously in *The Quiet Man*, starring Mau-reen O'Hara and John Wayne. The Irish were, for Ford, loquacious prototypes of another kind of western hero: hard drinking, quick to fight, loyal, antiestablishment, and suspicious of authority. Additionally, Ireland was a mythic place that represented home, and he would idealize "home" as a warm, safe haven presided over by a tough but loving matriarch in many of his films. In his adult life, however, that kind of home eluded him.

Ford did find a kind of surrogate home with Harry Carey and his wife, Olive, the silent screen actress. After Ford's older brother and first mentor, silent film actor and producer Frank Ford, brought Jack Feeney to Hollywood, gave him his start in the industry, and gave him his new name, Ford was taken under the wing of Harry Carey. It was Olive who'd first introduced Jack Ford to her husband; she'd met the young director on a Universal movie set when she was just sixteen. Harry persuaded Carl Laemmle, the head of Universal Studios, to hire Ford to direct his next Western.

Ford moved out to Carey's thousand-acre ranch north of Saugus, California—rugged country, though only thirty-five miles from Los Angeles—where Harry and Olive homesteaded their rustic ranch. Ford was a frequent live-in guest while learning his craft during the day making two-reeler Westerns for Universal. For Jack Ford, it was ideal.

"Pop was responsible for Ford being a director," wrote Carey's son, Harry "Dobe" Carey Jr., who would grow up to be a member of Ford's stock acting company. Dobe, nicknamed for the adobe-brick color of his hair, was born on the ranch in 1921 and spent his childhood there, which he remembered warmly: "Roaming the mountains and flatlands were coyotes, mountain lions, bobcats, and all the small game they hunted. . . . It was a place my father never wanted to leave. He always threw a fit when my mom told him he had to go to town." But of Jack Ford he was less nostalgic. "He scared the hell out of me," he wrote. "There was a cockiness about him that reminded me of the kids I'd wind up getting into fights with at school."

Apparently, the friendship soured between Ford and Carey, as Dobe later recalled: "He and my father were not working together anymore. I remember Pop being very happy about that." They made twenty-six movies together, splitting up in 1921 after making their final film, *Desperate Trails*, for Universal, but the years they had worked together were so important to them that Olive would refer to time "before Ford" and time "after Ford." Later, Ford described Harry Carey as "natural and rugged, but he had an innate modesty. He was a great, great actor, maybe the best Westerner ever," and declared that "Harry helped me immeasurably." But except for a small role in Ford's *Prisoner of Shark Island*, Carey never worked in a Ford film after 1921—even when the actor needed the work. When Dobe once asked his father why he never worked for Ford again, his father took a long drag on his cigarette and answered cryptically, "He won't ask me."

In many ways, though, the four years Ford spent as a young man making movies with Harry Carey and bunking down at his canyon mountain ranch were the happiest of his life. Whatever broke up that friendship, it started a pattern that would follow Ford professionally and personally from then on. Some biographers blame the split on Ford's resentment of Carey's higher salary; Dobe hints there was trouble on a more personal level. Whatever the reason, Ford was about to move from Universal to Fox Film Corporation, where he would eventually begin a long and rewarding—though sometimes contentious—relationship with the brilliant Darryl Zanuck, head of Fox Films. He'd learned a lot from Carey about visual storytelling, and he would try to re-create the magic he'd had with Carey with his next leading actor, another cowboy star, Hoot Gibson, but the magic couldn't be re-created.

Ford's personal life was equally rocky, a fact that his biographer Ronald Davis attributes, in part, to the class discrepancy between himself and his wife, Mary McBride Smith. Ford met Mary, suitably, at a St. Patrick's Day dance in 1920 at the Hollywood Hotel. Having moved on from Harry Carey, Ford was now making Westerns at Universal with his friend Hoot Gibson, with whom he was also sharing rooms. Mary was a Scotch-Irish Protestant from North Carolina, and apart from her youth and delicate beauty Ford was attracted to her pedigree. Her family had a naval background, which struck a chord with Ford's lifelong maritime obsession. Being turned down by the U.S. Naval Academy as a young man, probably for poor eyesight, failed to diminish his romantic attachment. More thrilling, perhaps, was the fact that Mary's grandfathers had been officers for the Confederacy, and she claimed that her family home had been burned down during Sherman's March. The sea and the military, especially the navy, dominated Ford's creative thinking, and making pictures was a way to satisfy those callings.

Jack and Mary were wed on July 3, 1920, soon after meeting, and set up household in a Beachwood Drive bungalow before settling into a stucco house on Odin Street, at the foot of the Hollywood Bowl. Though the house was relatively modest by Hollywood standards, they would live there for most of their married life, giving frequent parties that lasted until dawn. Their usual crowd was Ford's collection of movie actors, writers, and stuntmen, including Hoot Gibson and that other cowboy star, Tom Mix. The handsome silent film star George O'Brien was a frequent visitor, and even Hollywood royalty like Rudolph Valentino showed up one night and made a spaghetti dinner for everyone.

With their love of entertaining and Ford's success and clout in the film industry (his pictures always made money), they should have been happy. But Ford apparently believed that Mary felt superior to him; she was a member of both the Daughters of the American Revolution and the Daughters of the American Confederacy, whereas Ford was keenly aware of—and usually proud of—his origins as the son of Irish immigrants and the son of a saloon keeper. And like Duke's fiancée, Josephine, Mary was not especially interested in the motion picture business. To a woman of her class pretensions, there was something a little second-rate, even louche, about the trade; its moguls and big-shot directors were arrivistes. Ford asked his wife not to visit him on the sets of his pictures, and she had no problem complying with that request.

The conflicts inherent in their marriage were exacerbated by alcohol—lots and lots of alcohol. Ford, wrote Davis, "buried himself in work. He became more inward and stubborn, mixed crossness with affection, turned on people to assert himself, and lashed out at those he loved." Besides his obsession with work, his pleasure boat, the *Araner*, was an escape for him where he could devote himself to drink and male companionship, far from the blessings of civilization. It could get pretty debauched, however: Henry Fonda's son, the actor Peter Fonda, recalled that "Duke describe[d] how Ford would hole up on the *Araner* and get so drunk he would defecate on himself. He'd call out to the men on the boat to come down into his cabin, but no one would go down there into the hold, because it stank."

Despite his own excesses, Ford, as a student of American history, was intrigued by the idea of the American hero, and he set out to embody a series of mythic figures in his own life: a hard-drinking, feisty Irishman; a take-no-prisoners, successful director; a naval officer; a war hero; a patriot—a man's man. He did so in his dress, his speech, and his acts but, more important, through his movies and the heroes he helped bring to life on-screen: Harry Carey, George O'Brien, Henry Fonda, James Stewart, Tyrone Power, and—ultimately—John Wayne. Not only was he creating one of the greatest film legacies of the twentieth century; he was creating and re-creating himself, taking on the attributes of men he deeply admired. The burly actors Victor McLaglen and Ward Bond were, arguably, versions of his own blustery, outsized father.

But this process of self-mythology didn't lend itself to stability. After his fallout with Harry Carey, Ford bunked with Hoot Gibson for a while. He later bunked with the darkly handsome actor George O'Brien, whom he directed in the silent film *The Iron Horse*, one of the biggest moneymakers of the decade. These were intense relationships built on a kind of hero worship, involving mutually satisfying work, and then a bust-up followed by years of estrangement. He would repeat the pattern, on a smaller scale, with Duke Wayne after Duke defected to Raoul Walsh's camp when he made *The Big Trail*. But at least in Duke's case, Ford eventually rescued him from the period of obscure toil that followed his breakout role, and their professional and personal friendship flourished after that.

✳

After years of estrangement, one summer day in 1938 Ford spied his former third assistant property man fishing on the Long Beach Pier and invited him to come aboard the *Araner*, a ketch named after the Aran Islands. Soon after, Duke became a regular member of Ford's crew of actors, writers, and stuntmen invited on board Ford's beloved boat, spending weekends at Catalina Island. Ward Bond, Wayne's former classmate and now a veteran of several of Ford's films, was a frequent companion. Occasionally, they would drive down to San Pedro to drink and play poker. They often took fishing trips to Mexico, anchoring the *Araner* off the coast of Mazatlán, spending their evening drinking at the Hotel Belmar ("or one of the local whorehouses"). One New Year's Eve they proceeded to get so drunk that the Mexican *policía* demanded that they leave. These were riotous and heady times for Duke, but he had no illusions that his friendship with Ford would lead him back to working with the great director. "I never expected anything from Jack," Duke later said.

By now, Duke had persuaded Josephine to marry him. His difficult and apparently chaste six-year engagement culminated in their June 24, 1933, wedding in Bel Air, at the home of the actress Loretta Young. Duke declined to be confirmed as a Catholic, which sowed the seeds for unhappiness in a long marriage that would produce four children. Duke later told his third wife, Pilar, that those four conceptions were the product of the only times he and Josephine had had sex. Duke's long hours, usually from 5:00 a.m. to 7:30 p.m., strained the marriage further. He was often away for long periods on location shoots, and when he did come home at night, he was exhausted.

As the convent-raised daughter of a successful physician, Josephine was still the socialite, involved in charities and fund-raisers, and she resented her husband's unwillingness to share that part of her life. They quarreled often, and Josephine especially disliked the rough-and-tumble friends Duke liked to play poker with—

stuntmen who were also cowboys, wranglers, and rodeo men, with dust on their clothes and mud on their boots. Their third child, Patrick, was born in 1939, but the marriage had devolved beyond rescuing, and only their children and Josephine's Catholicism stood in the way of divorce. Duke was more than happy to spend time on Ford's yacht, away from home and family, in the company of men.

✻

When Ford began looking around for a charismatic actor to play the cowboy hero in his new film, the first Western he would make as a talkie, it never occurred to Duke to even ask to be considered for the part. Duke was humbled by the fifty-eight movies and serials he made for mostly second-rate studios; he felt there was something inherently second-rate about him, and he continued to revere Ford as an artist of the first order—an artist out of his own league.

But the role of the Ringo Kid in Ford's new picture was perfect for John Wayne—a charismatic outlaw who becomes the moral center and hero of the story in the tradition of the "good bad man"—and it was the role that could rescue him from Monogram-Republic obscurity. On board the *Araner* one weekend in the summer of 1938, while fishing off Catalina Island, Ford teased the now seasoned young actor, asking him to recommend someone else for the part. "I'm having a hell of a time deciding whom to cast as the Ringo Kid," he said. "You know a lot of young actors, Duke. See what you think."

He tossed the script over to Duke. Dudley Nichols and Ben Hecht had adapted a 1937 *Collier's* magazine story titled "Stage to Lordsburg" by Ernest Haycox, and Ford's rather beleaguered son Patrick, who was then working as his father's production assistant, brought it to Ford's attention. The producer Walter Wanger wanted Gary Cooper for the sympathetic role of a young gunfighter who breaks out of jail after a dubious conviction in order to avenge the deaths of his father and brother. But Ford felt that Cooper was too old for the part, and too expensive for the half-million-dollar budget. It was the second time that the lanky actor, star of *High Noon*, was jettisoned to make way for John Wayne.

Ever willing to please Ford, who seemed content just to have Duke as a drinking buddy on fishing trips, Duke offered up the actor Lloyd Nolan as a possibility. Ford seemed to mull over Duke's suggestion and didn't mention it again until they docked at San Pedro. He finally turned to Duke and said, "You idiot. Couldn't you play it?"

Ford later explained in a characteristic understatement, "When the time came for me to do 'Stagecoach' I thought about Duke. [Walter] Wanger was producing the picture, and he never interfered with my casting. We took a test of him in Western clothes, just to get an idea—not a moving test but a still camera test. He looked great. Wanger liked him to play the part. The rest is history. Duke went from there to bigger things."

STAGECOACHED

The story of *Stagecoach* couldn't be simpler: a society in microcosm barrels across the New Mexico Territory in 1885 in order to reach Lordsburg without being attacked by warring Apaches. It's an ensemble piece in which characters are brought together in close quarters, where their best and worst selves are revealed. Each of the passengers in the stagecoach, driven by Andy Devine as Buck, with the marshal, Curly (George Bancroft), riding shotgun, has a compelling reason to take the dangerous trip. A disgraced, alcoholic doctor played by veteran character actor Thomas Mitchell, one of Ford's favorite Irish American actors, rides cheek by jowl with a whiskey salesman, played by Donald Meek. Mitchell's character is arguably a stand-in for John Ford himself—an Irish drunk who is able to pull himself together to deliver a baby, just as the heavy-drinking Ford pulled himself together again and again to deliver a movie, on time and on budget. Mitchell would win an Academy Award for Best Supporting Actor for his performance.

The cast is rounded out by John Carradine as a southern gambler named Hatfield whose gallantry in escorting Lucy Mallory, a young cavalry officer's pregnant wife played by Louise Platt, nearly redeems his shady past as a gunfighter who once shot a man in the back. An outwardly respectable banker named Gatewood, played by Berton Churchill, turns out to be a thief absconding with funds, in part to escape his overbearing wife. The very presence of the town prostitute, Dallas, played by Claire Trevor, is a thumb in the eye of more "respectable" travelers, except for the Ringo Kid—John Wayne—an honest outlaw as natural and noble as the wind-carved landscape through which their stagecoach rolls. He falls in love with her.

Released in 1939, *Stagecoach* is widely considered the first Western made for adult entertainment. It is also Ford's first movie to be partly filmed in the starkly beautiful Monument Valley along the southwestern border of Arizona and Utah, a locale he would often return to and that gave his Westerns a grandeur and austerity unseen in Westerns before Ford and influencing how Westerns would be filmed thereafter. In *Stagecoach*, Ford introduces—or reintroduces—Duke to the public with a flourish. As a young outlaw who has escaped prison to hunt down the men who killed his father and brother, he is the embodiment of the "good bad man," an outlaw whose basic goodness shines forth from his open countenance and whose straightforwardness and courtesy extend even to Dallas, the shunned prostitute aboard the stagecoach.

Ringo hails the stagecoach halfway to Lordsburg because his horse has gone lame, and Ford practically stops the film to register his presence. The camera frames him in a long shot, slightly out of focus as if to tease the viewer, then zooms in to capture his handsome Scotch-Irish face and admire his torso, languidly posed against the vast background landscape. We see that Duke's face is no longer young—certainly not young enough to still be con-

✳

Stagecoach, 1939: A stagecoach barrels through majestic
Monument Valley. "The real star of my Westerns has always
been the land," Ford once said.

sidered "the Kid"—but his innocent friendliness gives him youth. He's immediately greeted by Buck, the driver, happy to see his old friend, who shouts, "Hey, it's Ringo!" Once Ringo has boarded the stagecoach, Buck tells the marshal, "Ain't Ringo a fine boy!" The marshal, who has just confiscated Ringo's rifle and virtually put him under arrest for his unlawful escape, says a bit grudgingly, "I think so." Right away we know that Ringo is a good man regardless of the law's opinion.

This goodness derives, in part, from the very fact that he *is* an outlaw, someone isolated from the stultifying strictures of civilization represented by the Law and Order League, scolding women who have driven Dallas out of town. In his private life, Ford lampooned such reform-minded leagues, calling his cadre of drinking buddies on board the *Araner* the "Young Men's Purity, Total Abstinence, and Snooker Pool Club." It's worth noting that reform-minded women of the era devoted themselves to, among other things, the prohibition of alcohol, prostitution, and gambling— three vices that loom large in all Westerns in the form of the frontier saloon. The townswomen are portrayed as pinched harridans and hags, in marked contrast to Dallas's youth and beauty. She is Ringo's counterpart as the good "bad" woman, the whore with the heart of gold.

A family-loving man, Ringo is out to avenge his father and brother. He is righteous in his devotion not just to family honor but to restoring justice more broadly, attested to by his willingness to return to prison and serve out the rest of his sentence once the deed is done. As the feminist film critic Joan Mellen has pointed out, "What already counts for the Wayne character is principle, never personal comfort." Facets of the later John Wayne persona emerge from his "sweet and open" face—a steely hardness when he describes the murder of his father and brother and what he intends to do about it. And, though shackled, he leads the weaker men aboard the stagecoach, intervening in a fight between the gambler Hatfield and the drunken doctor and heroically fending off attacking Apaches from the top of the stagecoach. Later, when Dallas

＊

Duke Wayne as the Ringo Kid and Claire Trevor as Dallas
in 1939's *Stagecoach*. Whether or not Ringo knows
Dallas is a prostitute, he loves her just the same.

urges him to make his escape, Ringo refuses because "there are some things a man can't run away from." That statement foreshadows the John Wayne hero who will capture audiences in many films to come.

Ringo's genuine courtesy toward the stagecoach passengers includes the outcast Dallas, a contrast to the phony, flowery courtesy of Hatfield, the southern gambler, who only shows respect to Lucy Mallory, the cavalry officer's wife, with whom he is smitten and with whom he shares the lost cause of the Confederacy. When Hatfield offers Lucy a drink from a silver cup but refuses one to Dallas, Ringo rescues her from humiliation and gives her a drink from the only canteen of water. He offers water all around before taking a drink himself, a measure of his selflessness. And when they make their first stop at a roadside outpost, the Ringo Kid seeks the company of Dallas after the gambler and the officer's wife have snubbed her by refusing to eat at the same table. Ringo insists that all the passengers treat Dallas with respect.

That Ringo perceives her essential goodness evokes our sympathy. But does he recognize Dallas as the shamed woman she is, having missed seeing her run out of town? Played with Claire Trevor's usual rueful wit, Dallas is surprised and touched by Ringo's attentions to her. Noticing that the other passengers refuse to sit with her at the dining table, Ringo assumes it's *he* who's being shunned, because he is, after all, an outlaw just broken out of jail. Whether Ringo knows her social status or not is a question that Ford and Wayne don't answer. All we know is that Ringo's gallantry turns to love over the course of their journey, and Dallas, cynical and self-protective at first, eventually accepts that she is worthy of being loved. They run off together at the film's end, to Ringo's homestead in Mexico, a place of redemption beyond the dubious "blessings of civilization" and the vice and danger of the coach's ironically named destination, Lordsburg. Only in the wildness of the territory beyond the border will Ringo and Dallas truly be free.

The Western hero seeks freedom, to live life on his own

terms, even if it means leaving civilization behind, as Ringo does. His Mexican homestead is a place "where a man can *live*—and a *wo*man," he tells Dallas. This early incarnation of the John Wayne hero possesses a blend of innocence and resolve, an ability to trust his instincts beyond the dictates of society, an ability to experience love for a woman and to act on that emotion—to protect but not to control. His line to Dallas evokes the lines from *War of the Wildcats* that Joan Didion remembered with such wistfulness: that he would build her a house "at the bend in the river where the cottonwoods grow."

But in later Ford-Wayne Westerns, as the masculine hero evolves, the woman will be all but dropped from the equation.

⁂

After almost ten years in the wilderness, before *Stagecoach*, Duke had considered himself nearly over-the-hill, more stuntman than actor. Now that he was back in a real, grown-up movie again, he felt he had a lot of catching up to do. Veteran character actor and friend Paul Fix, who would go on to play Marshal Micah Torrance in *The Rifleman*, agreed to coach him in the role. Though Duke's delivery is still somewhat stilted compared with that of more experienced actors like Claire Trevor and Thomas Mitchell, Duke managed to turn his liabilities to his favor. It would take him years to learn how to deliver a line with unstudied ease, but from the outset he possessed a powerful and graceful physical presence. His embodiment of Ringo—the way he twirls the Winchester and then tosses it up, one-handed, to the marshal; the way he folds his tall, muscular frame into the cramped space of the stagecoach; the stunts he performs, created and sometimes doubled by his friend Yakima Canutt, whom Duke brought into the production—speaks to his easy strength. What he would discover, though, was that throughout his career, his lack of theatrical polish would only deepen his authenticity and his popularity, especially with audiences who are suspicious of artifice. His very stiffness as an actor would underline the notion that Duke really *was* the heroic character he played in the movie; in Duke's world, to adopt the smooth, versatile delivery of the virtuoso was a bit suspect—let the easterners flaunt their technique.

TASKMASTER

With the two men united in their vision for the role of the Ringo Kid, and with Ford having lobbied to cast Duke in the part, filming should have been a pleasurable collaboration. Instead, it was hell.

Ford, who had already developed a reputation as a pitiless taskmaster given to bouts of cruelty, rode Duke without mercy during the first three weeks of filming. It had happened with other actors before. On the set of *The Iron Horse*, Ford physically attacked his older brother, Eddie O'Fearna, whom he'd employed as his second assistant on the picture. Later, he punched Henry Fonda, one of his favorite actors, on the set of *Mister Roberts*, which ended their working relationship. Dobe Carey described the day John Ford knelt on his back and broke one of his ribs on the set of *Two Rode Together*, angry that Dobe had shown up hungover. Despite his own heavy drinking, Ford kept a no-alcohol-while-filming rule for everyone involved in the picture—a necessity in order for Ford to even undertake the job.

If Ford had "a happy childhood," as he claimed, did his penchant for cruelty derive from some unresolved conflict within himself? Like many tough men, he could be sentimental, and indeed his films have been faulted, and also celebrated, for their sentimentality. But it's almost as if the tough side and the sensitive side could not meet. He was a football hero in high school, which he trumpeted to hide his "sensitive side," the part of him that loved to draw, that read history and fiction. He would make cruel fun of the heavy-featured Ward Bond, even sketching caricatures of the rugged actor as a gorilla, but later he would disparage his own appearance, saying, "I myself am a pretty ugly fellow—no one would pay to see me onscreen."

Given his preference for and celebration of male camaraderie, both in life and on film, it seems Ford worked extra hard at dispelling any suggestion of homosexuality—a career killer—which might have motivated his autocratic, often cruel behavior toward his actors. And then there was alcohol. Ford never touched a drop when he was making a picture, but between pictures he was a binge drinker, given to blackouts. When he wasn't drinking, he could charm the birds from the trees. He flourished in an era when alcohol flowed freely in Hollywood—even during Prohibition—and was not considered a potential poison. Indeed, the prevailing attitude among Ford and his circle was never to trust a man who *didn't* drink. Being able to hold one's liquor, and to drink prodigiously, was another way to earn one's masculine bona fides.

Ford's wife, Mary, recalled the Hollywood parties Ford would throw at their home at 6860 Odin Street. "They were all hard drinkers," Mary once said in an interview, and Ford encouraged everyone at his parties to kick back and imbibe. During Prohibition, Ford had a secret drinking room hidden by a sliding door where he kept his cache of liquor.

Ford's sobriety at work didn't blunt his innate penchant for cruelty. On the set of *Stagecoach*, he made a special point of belittling Duke, who was already insecure in the presence of his more experienced fellow actors. At one point he grabbed Duke's chin and asked, "Why are you moving your mouth so much? Don't you know that you don't act with your mouth in pictures? You act with your eyes!" He repeatedly called Duke "a big oaf" and "a dumb bastard," at one point yelling at him, "Can't you walk, instead of skipping like a goddamn fairy?" That insult might have been pure projection, because Olive Carey had once described John Ford as having a distinctly effeminate walk, and Duke himself has often said that he learned that graceful, slow-rolling gait from Ford. In Ford's world, to call someone a "fairy" or a "pansy" was the greatest insult he could muster.

But Wayne endured it. And he continued to look up to Ford and admire the older man's abilities as a director, grateful that

A jaunty John Ford at the top of his game, 1939.

Ford had, at the last moment, opened the doors to a big career. He would later defend Ford's mistreatment of him:

> When we first started *Stagecoach*, he rode me unmercifully; and it became quite obvious why he did. I was his friend, I was unknown in the business; he had top actors—[Thomas] Mitchell, [John] Carradine, Claire [Trevor], people who are well known in the business; and despite of the fact I'd been a star for 10 years in children's pictures, you know, I wasn't part of the colony. And he did not want them to resent me. . . . [P]eople would start to say, "stop picking on him" so they tried to help me instead of resenting me. That's the only time that I can ever remember him unmercifully riding me.

But the abuse was so palpable the other actors asked Ford to lighten up on the newcomer. Duke endured it because he felt that Ford was forcing him to reach beyond himself and grow as an actor, the way a coach pushes his players to their limit; he was also keenly aware that "Jack Ford stood up for me on so many occasions" and that he owed his developing career to the pugnacious director.

With *Stagecoach* a critical and financial success, Duke realized he could have more say in his next picture, and he confided to Harry Carey's wife, Olive, that he'd like to do something along the lines of *The White Company*, a novel set in the age of chivalry and knighthood. "You are a big, dumb son of a bitch," she reportedly told him. "The people have told you how they like you. They're your audience. You give them what they want, not what you want."

It didn't matter. Despite his stellar turn in *Stagecoach*, Duke found himself back in the salt mines, toiling again for Republic in a series of mostly forgettable Westerns: *The Night Riders*, *Three Texas Steers*, *Wyoming Outlaw*, *New Frontier*, *Allegheny Uprising* (this one for RKO Pictures), and *Dark Command*, which reunited him with Raoul Walsh. Finally, Ford rescued him once again, in the 1940 film for United Artists *The Long Voyage Home*.

In another drama of men without women, this time aboard

a tramp steamer at the outset of World War II, Duke has a small supporting role as an innocent, young Norwegian sailor, with a creditable accent, aboard a steamer, with an ensemble cast headed, again, by Thomas Mitchell. It was a different kind of role for Duke, far from the mold of the Western hero he was becoming known for, but it drew on the openhearted innocence that Duke still possessed.

3 GODFATHERS

It's not until Ford's 1948 Western *3 Godfathers*, made for Argosy Pictures/MGM nine years after *Stagecoach*, that Duke Wayne comes across the screen as the full-fledged, larger-than-life John Wayne of the popular imagination.

In *3 Godfathers*, Duke is now a mature man, heavy in the torso but still light on his feet, his youthful beauty hardened into a face of experience and resolve. The innocence is gone, and in its place is an unmistakable authority, a bracing masculine presence. This is a hero born to command, yet tempered by concern for those weaker than himself. As a bank robber on the lam who nonetheless acts honorably throughout the picture, he again embodies the "good bad man."

The story is an allegorical retelling of the biblical tale of the three wise men, set in the West, and adapted by Frank S. Nugent and Laurence Stallings from a novelette, *3 Godfathers*, by Peter B. Kyne. The three godfathers are desperadoes, having just robbed a bank in the small desert town of Welcome, Arizona, and are now being chased through the unforgiving desert by the town's sheriff, Perley "Buck" Sweet, played by the gruff and likable Ward Bond. As the outlaws, Robert "Bob" Hightower, William Kearney, a.k.a. the Abilene Kid, and Pedro, search for water in the desert, they come across a dying woman, who they later learn is the sheriff's sister-in-law. Abandoned by her husband, she is about to give birth. They come to her aid—clumsily, abashedly—and she asks them to promise to take care of her infant, whom she names Robert Wil-

✳

The three outlaws rescue and protect an infant,
discovering their feminine sides.

liam Pedro, after the three bank robbers. It's nearly Christmas Eve, and as it happens, the nearest town is New Jerusalem, where they decide to bring the infant after the Abilene Kid stumbles across a Bible passage that seems to instruct them.

Only John Ford could pull off a biblical allegory in the form of a Western.

It's clear that the Abilene Kid has received some kind of divine message—not just because he finds their direction in the Bible, but because Ford lights his face in such a way that his blue eyes take on an otherworldly illumination and he appears for a moment like a saint from a stained-glass window. It's anything but subtle. But then we have John Wayne as the scoffer, who says early that it will be a long time before he "gets religion" and whose gruff realism bracingly offsets the religious sentimentality. Pedro, the Mexican bandito played with gusto by Pedro Armendáriz, is the most macho of the three, and his frequent making of the sign of the cross also undercuts his machismo.

Though the movie is at times mawkish and heavy-handed in its allegorical symbolism, it's a satisfying and enjoyable picture, and a story that clearly moved Ford. He had filmed it once before, in 1919, as a silent film called *Marked Men,* starring his friend, mentor, and cowboy hero, Harry Carey. In fact, *3 Godfathers* is dedicated to the memory of Ford's onetime friend, who died the previous year, in 1947; and his son, Dobe Carey, appears as the Abilene Kid, the youngest of the three bank robbers. Duke Wayne as Bob Hightower, the leader of the desperadoes, comes across as a reincarnation of Harry Carey. He's dressed like the silent film star, wearing a Union soldier shirt with an ever present neckerchief and "Texas" hat, his hair slicked down the same way; when resting, he leans back in a pose reminiscent of Carey.

The three outlaws, toting their infant charge, struggle to make it to New Jerusalem through punishing desert sands and salt flats while running out of water and jettisoning their horses and saddles. Two of them don't make it. The Abilene Kid succumbs to an injury, having been shot in the shoulder during their escape, and Pedro breaks his leg and is left with a pistol to finish himself off—we hear the lone gunshot in the distance. Only the strongest of the three, Duke's Bob Hightower, makes it to New Jerusalem, where the infant is rescued. Hightower, though, is arrested by Sheriff Sweet, whose posse has been trailing him through the desert.

Next we see two men enjoying a game of chess in Hightower's prison cell. The sheriff and his wife are so grateful that he's saved their infant nephew that all is forgiven. Sheriff Sweet has always liked Bob—"The more I think about that big fella in the Texas hat," he says early in the film, "the more I admire him." He's impressed by Hightower's cleverness during the escape, and of course he's moved by the outlaw's vow to take care of the infant to honor its mother's last wish. Bob is sentenced to one year and one day in jail for bank robbery, a reduced sentence to reward his refusal to renege on his promise to the infant's mother. As Hightower, handcuffed to a deputy whom he practically drags behind him, is put on the train to prison, the town organizes a fond send-off. The local beauty, who happens to be the bank president's daughter, makes a promise on behalf of the townspeople to welcome him back. Clearly, all is forgiven, because this is a man who risked his life and freedom to keep a sacred promise.

Unlike in *The Big Trail* and *Stagecoach*, however, Duke Wayne does not get the girl in *3 Godfathers*. Though there's a hint of a possible future romance, the real emotional bond is between the three desperadoes, who carry out their mission with loyalty and cooperation. Then there's the relationship between Robert Hightower and Sheriff Sweet, a burly guy whose feminine name produces guffaws from the three outlaws, as does Bob Hightower's fancy, effeminate middle name, Marmaduke. Playing chess in the local jail, then being served dinner by the sheriff's wife, the two men are downright cozy. So the cowboy hero, as shaped by John Ford, begins to evolve from an outlaw with innate goodness who woos and wins the girl to one tough hombre, true to his word, who will find his greatest satisfaction in the company of other men.

*

Duke Wayne, Harry Carey Jr., and Pedro
Armendáriz as desperadoes in 3 *Godfathers*, 1948.

3 Godfathers is not the first or last film in which Ford softens the toughness of his Western hero by having him perform maternal duties, albeit with clumsiness and resistance. The scene in which Duke Wayne greases down the newborn in axle grease, following the dictates of a nineteenth-century baby book they've found among the dead mother's belongings, is funny but weirdly unsettling. As Wayne applies thick yellow goo to the baby's bare bottom, Ford lavishes a lot of attention on the scene. It's as if to say that the masculine hero doesn't need the help of a woman; he can get the job done himself, no matter how ham-handedly. It's also Ford's way of combining two opposing realms: the coziness of domesticity and the wild open spaces of the masculine Western. Domesticity when practiced by men is comic but comforting. When practiced by women, however, it can be a shackle on the spirit of their men: when he's home with his wife, Sheriff Sweet is pruning roses. He only achieves a masculine presence when he reveals his sheriff's badge and commands a posse in search of the three bank robbers.

Despite the comic, almost cringe-worthy baby-greasing scene, in *3 Godfathers* we have all the elements that make up the archetypal American hero, circa 1948. There's toughness as Duke and his comrades survive a sandstorm and the trek through the desert with scant water; protectiveness toward the weak when Duke carries the infant or makes sure the Abilene Kid, barely out of his teens, doesn't do any of the shooting during the robbery and gets most of the dwindling water in the canteen; the keeping of promises when Duke would rather go to prison than break his word to the infant's dying mother. All are embodied by John Wayne, no matter that he plays an unrepentant bank robber. These were also the hallmarks of America's self-image, carried through its foreign policy, throughout the World War II era: toughness, protectiveness, and the keeping of promises. Ford would explore these themes further in three important Westerns, a trilogy of films about the Seventh Cavalry.

3

Soldier's Joy: The Cavalry Trilogy

To me he was sort of like Moses. But I feared him in a good way.
—RODDY MCDOWALL ON JOHN FORD

In the military, we love our legends.
—LIEUTENANT GENERAL DANIEL P. BOLGER, U.S. ARMY, RETIRED

Soldier's Joy" is the title of an Appalachian fiddler's tune, originally Scottish, dating from the 1760s. During the American
Civil War, the melody gained lyrics, with "soldier's joy" acting as
a euphemism for the mix of whiskey, beer, and morphine given
to grievously wounded soldiers: "Gimme some of that Soldier's
Joy, you know what I mean / I don't want to hurt no more my
leg is turnin' green." But when applied to John Ford's movies, the
phrase describes the joy of camaraderie and shared purpose and
the pleasures of men living alongside men, close to the natural
world—pleasures that Ford especially celebrates in his Cavalry
Trilogy, filmed between 1947 and 1950, and that he sought to re-
create on location with his stock company of actors, stuntmen,
and crew in the expansive wildernesses of Monument Valley and
Moab, Utah. Ford's firsthand experience of these pleasures dated

back to his wartime service, perhaps the most formative and influential period of his life.

Despite significant success in the movie business, Ford had never overcome his youthful disappointment at not getting into the U.S. Naval Academy and joining the navy; life aboard the *Araner* was a kind of compensation, a chance to command a small ship at sea, crewed by his friends and drinking buddies. In 1939, with the stirrings of war threatening, Captain Ellis Zacharias, a chief intelligence officer of the Eleventh Naval District, asked Ford to use his fishing excursions to Mexico aboard the *Araner* to take note of the presence of Japanese fishing boats in the area and report back. Already a member of the U.S. Navy Reserve, Ford was thrilled at the covert assignment. He took his command seriously, spying on the fishing vessels and charting their locations, certain that the boats were not the innocent trawlers they appeared to be. He reported back to Zacharias, "The Japanese shrimp fleet was lying at anchor. It is my belief that the crews and officers of this shrimp fleet belong to the Imperial Navy or Reserve. The crews are not the same class of fishermen that I have seen so many times in Japan."

Ford had always longed for opportunities to prove his masculinity. With the coming war, he now had his chance to be a hero using the very thing he knew best and excelled at: making motion pictures. At the invitation of William "Wild Bill" Donovan, the highly decorated head of the newly formed Office of the Coordinator of Information (precursor of the CIA), Ford deployed his skills making newsreels and short films to boost navy morale. In 1940, Ford and Donovan created the wartime Field Photographic Division, recruiting cinematographer Gregg Toland, film editor Robert Parrish, and writers Budd Schulberg and Garson Kanin. Sensing that America would enter the fray, Ford planned to use the newly established unit to photograph frontline combat for newsreel coverage.

With that in mind, the Photographic Division went into training, renting uniforms from Western Costume and borrowing props from 20th Century Fox. Ford was an expert in the pomp and ceremony of military units, which he would put to great use in his Cavalry Trilogy at the end of the 1940s, and organizing the uniforms, the drills, and the combat matériel gave him immense satisfaction. Ford's Field Photographic Division was quickly given official status by the U.S. Navy and Washington, though its first assignment was a far cry from Ford's heroic ideal. In one case he was asked to create a thirty-minute public service film called *Sex Hygiene* to warn military recruits of the perils of venereal disease.

The film short was released in 1942 by 20th Century Fox, and by showing graphic images of the ravages of syphilis, it recommended abstinence as the best preventative. (In a curious footnote, one of the GIs cast in the film was the strapping actor George Reeves, who would go on to fame, and a tragic end, as television's first Superman in *Adventures of Superman*.) The film's editor, Gene Fowler Jr., recalled, "Ford just loved it! The army would send these guys up under guard for him to photograph, and I think he took a perverse pleasure in showing this shocking stuff." When *Sex Hygiene* was shown to draftees at Fort MacArthur, "They had guys running out and throwing up."

＊

But by no means had Ford abandoned Hollywood filmmaking during this period. He won an Academy Award for Best Director for 1940's *The Grapes of Wrath*, an adaptation of John Steinbeck's novel about migrant workers during the Great Depression. And he followed that up the next year with Richard Llewellyn's *How Green Was My Valley*, which he took over from director William Wyler, another celebration of working-class struggle set among miners in Wales. It's worth noting that this was the first time Ford worked with two actresses he came to love and admire, Maureen O'Hara and Anna Lee, though he showed it in his usual combative and sometimes brutal style. Anna Lee had failed to tell her director that she was pregnant with twins when filming began, afraid he wouldn't use her if he knew. At one of the film's climaxes, when her character, Bronwyn, learns of her husband's death, she screams and falls to the ground. The night after shooting that scene, Anna Lee suffered a miscarriage and lost one of the twins. She and Ford were both devastated, yet she continued to work with him and continued to be grateful for every John Ford movie she appeared in—as did Maureen O'Hara, despite her own problems with the director. One wonders if there was a kind of Stockholm syndrome at play in which the bullied and mistreated cast and crew identified with and forgave their abuser, or if the actors were so thrilled to achieve the artistic heights Ford brought out in them that such accomplishment was worth any price.

As a child actor, Roddy McDowall had already appeared in twenty British films; his memory of being directed by the great, tyrannical Ford was mostly benign: "The thing that sticks out about *How Green Was My Valley* is that I never remember being directed. It just all happened. Ford played me like a harp." Even so, McDowall remembers that he was "scared to death of him."

> To me he was sort of like Moses. But I feared him in a good way. He was religion to me in a certain sense, which touched me and released me and did not inhibit me. Ford could be just terrible. If he chose to, he could destroy you in a minute. But he was marvelous to me.

Ford would win his third Academy Award for Best Director for *How Green Was My Valley*, and the movie beat *Citizen Kane* in being awarded the Oscar for Best Picture. But by that time Ford was already on to other, and to his mind better, things. In September 1941, while at the top of his game as a director and producer of motion pictures, Ford had realized his childhood dream by entering active service in the U.S. Navy. As head of the Field Photographic Branch (the later name of the unit), Ford was stationed in June 1942 at Midway, where he was asked to film footage of young recruits going about their daily business on the base. Word came down that the Japanese were planning to attack, and Ford, who was lounging in his bunk at the time, quickly rose to the occasion and filmed the air battle with a 16 mm, handheld camera, sustaining shrapnel wounds while he filmed. He already had footage of many of the sailors and marines, so he was able to put together an eighteen-minute documentary, *The Battle of Midway*, on this pivotal engagement and on the men who fought in it, some of whom lost their lives.

Ford knew that without an intimate story his film would be seen as mere propaganda or—worse, still—be censored by the military, so he used his narrative gifts to assemble a folksy look at young men in battle, fresh from their Ohio farms. The motherly Jane Darwell, who played the tough matriarch in *The Grapes of Wrath* just two years earlier, served as one of several narrators. In a "land sakes alive" voice, she identifies the young men—"why, isn't that Junior Kenney from Springfield, Ohio?"—while Donald Crisp, who played the loving father in *How Green Was My Valley*, provided the complementary voice of a warm, loving patriarch. Henry Fonda also lent his voice to the homey tribute to the young men in battle. The voice-over narration is a little corny to contemporary ears, but the juxtaposition of these down-home American voices against the eerie, menacing beauty of bombs detonating in air—billowing black clouds of smoke slowly drifting over the Pacific—is indeed moving.

But none of this recording was formally sanctioned by the military. When Ford returned to Los Angeles on June 18, 1942, he practically had to smuggle the footage into the country so that he could edit it before the navy brass could intervene, because there was concern that the footage showed the navy as unprepared for battle. Ford cleverly spliced in footage of Franklin D. Roosevelt's son James, who was serving in the Pacific as a Marine Corps officer; when the eighteen-minute documentary was shown to the president, Roosevelt made sure that "every mother in America" would see the film uncensored. And Ford won his first Academy Award for Best Documentary, a new category created that year.

Moved by the men he saw killed in action, Ford made another

documentary short, this time an eight-minute tribute to the twenty-nine men (out of thirty) of Torpedo Squadron Eight who had died or were missing in action. He identified each man by name and sent copies of the 8mm film, called simply *Torpedo Squadron 8*, to all of the families of the deceased.

Looking over Ford's body of work, critics have noted that his wartime experience gave him the increased confidence to ignore public taste and follow his own inclinations. Film historian Mark Harris makes a similar point about John Huston and George Stevens, writing of the three men,

> Their experiences during the war had strengthened their resolve to let nothing compromise their work, not even popular taste. . . . Ford, ever iconoclastic, chose to eschew the prestige of films like *The Grapes of Wrath* and instead embrace the degraded genre he loved best, shaping his own vision of America through the majestic, elegiac, morally complex westerns that, though they would win him no awards, would eventually form his most enduring legacy.

But Ford had always followed his own instincts from the very beginning, willing to do battle with studio moguls whenever necessary. More to the point, his wartime naval experience, as well as his work filming alongside young fighting men he admired and came to know personally, was the most deeply satisfying period in a life studded with adventures, honors, and awards. And it was the ethos cultivated among fighting men that he would channel into the Cavalry Trilogy.

FORT APACHE

Fort Apache was filmed in Monument Valley, in scenes visually reminiscent of *Stagecoach*. It profoundly illustrates the meaning of honor, duty, and sacrifice and what it means to belong to a cadre of men, set against a landscape so immense in scale it both dwarfs

men's accomplishments and sets them in a mythological frame-
work. Ford didn't set out to film a trilogy, but the three Westerns—
Fort Apache, She Wore a Yellow Ribbon, and *Rio Grande,* released
between 1948 and 1950—all depict the struggles and challenges
of the Seventh Cavalry division of the U.S. Army during the
Indian wars from 1866 to 1881. Specific characters link these
films as well: Duke plays Captain Kirby York in *Fort Apache* and
returns as the promoted Lieutenant Colonel Kirby Yorke (with
an added *e*) in *Rio Grande,* while Sergeant Quincannon appears
in all three. And all of the trilogy Westerns were based on *Saturday Evening Post* short stories by the Western writer James Warner
Bellah.

Bellah's stories were militaristic and jingoistic, racist in their
depictions of Native Americans. "My father was an absolute military snob," James Bellah Jr. said about his father. "His politics were
just a little right of Attila. He was a fascist, a racist, and a world-
class bigot." Bellah's bigotry even extended to John Ford, whom
he considered "a shanty Irishman." He hated Hollywood, which he
characterized as "full of Jews and crass commoners," and he made
no bones about being in it for the money. It's interesting that Ford
was drawn to Bellah's stories for their subject matter and their
cinematic qualities, but to his credit he backed away from Bellah's
depiction of Indians as rapacious killers.

Further exploring Ford's obsession with American history and
tales of western conquest, *Fort Apache* was adapted from Bellah's
1947 short story "Massacre," but Ford clearly incorporates other
allusions, particularly George Armstrong Custer's disastrous Battle of Little Bighorn against the Sioux nation. Frank S. Nugent
wrote the screenplay, which was nominated by the Writers Guild
of America for a best screenplay award and which began a collaboration that would span eleven films. Nugent well knew that his
screenplay was just the scaffolding for Ford and that Ford would
provide much of the dialogue and dispense with exposition wherever possible. Ford was famous for ripping out pages of dialogue
in his shooting scripts, and Nugent realized that "the writer had

better keep out of his way. The finished picture is always Ford's, never the writer's."

This was true in nearly every aspect of Ford's filmmaking. He took great pains, for example, to achieve a specific costume aesthetic even if it meant abandoning historical accuracy. When Bellah complained that "on the frontier, the troops didn't wear those sloppy hats on garrison duty," Ford reportedly looked him in the eye and answered, "They do now." The cavalry hat turned up in the front was Ford's invention. "The main thing with a Western is hats," he believed. "If you have decent hats on people their character will come through."

Ford's deepest sense of belonging and satisfaction was working with those core members of his stock company—screenwriter Dudley Nichols, Ward Bond, Victor McLaglen, Dobe Carey, and, of course, Duke Wayne. Except for Anna Lee and Maureen O'Hara, it was a mostly male club with its own rituals, rules, expectations, and punishments. Happy unions between men and women are few and occur early in Ford's oeuvre, increasingly replaced by the celebration of male camaraderie. Especially in his Cavalry Trilogy and his World War II movies, such as *They Were Expendable* and *The Wings of Eagles*, army life is presented as a preferable alternative to traditional marriage, a paean to male nobility, cohesiveness, sacrifice, and ritual, with little romance but lots of comic relief thrown in. These films are strongly homosocial—men working and living together in harmony—and what we might identify today as man-crushes or bromances abound, but homosexuality is unrealized and unspoken. Only glimpses filter through in some of the horseplay among men, including the extended brawls usually initiated by Victor McLaglen.

Jack Donovan, the conservative extoller of hyper-masculinity, wrote, "Masculinity is about being a man within a group of men. Above all things, masculinity is about what men want from each other." But because these are John Ford movies, the toughness of men living and fighting alongside men is softened by touches of domesticity and humor, often achieved by feminizing the burliest and most pugnacious actor. In *3 Godfathers*, Ward Bond is wearing an apron and spritzing the roses when we first see him, and Duke Wayne clumsily diapers, feeds, and protects a newborn. In all three cavalry movies, Ford's reliable character actor and favorite stock Irishman, Victor McLaglen, an ex-prizefighter who matched Wayne in sheer size and physical presence, supplies those lighter touches with comic drunkenness.

Ford's interest in feminizing his heroes often pairs with an interest in order and structure. *Fort Apache* celebrates a certain kind of necessary order and the ritualistic observance of that order, beginning with its opening shots of the outpost's officers and NCOs at a formal dance with their wives. Ford's movies almost always include indigenous music and often include dancing, which serves two purposes: to illustrate the beauty and communal cohesiveness of formally choreographed movement, and to show, sometimes comically but often gracefully, tough men in the feminine act of dancing.

In Ford's *My Darling Clementine*, filmed two years before *Fort Apache*, lean, crane-like Henry Fonda dances stiffly, and he would be a comic figure if it were not for the solemnity he employs as he dances, or rather marches, his mate across the floor. In *Fort Apache*, bulky Ward Bond and towering John Wayne are surprisingly graceful on their feet. Their physical grace and courtliness toward the women living on the outpost mark them as superior men, able to fulfill the masculine requirements of their military calling but also willing to participate in—and enjoy!—the civilizing activity of dance. Through niceties of social behavior and dancing skill, Ford manages to feminize his manliest characters, rescuing them from stereotype. Or, looked at another way, real men *do* dance.

In *Fort Apache*, John Wayne portrays Captain Kirby York, an admired Civil War veteran who is replaced as Fort Apache's commander by West Point veteran Lieutenant Colonel Owen Thursday, played by Henry Fonda. Thursday—a character roughly based on the infamous and ill-fated George Custer—has been demoted

✳

Henry Fonda as Lieutenant Colonel Owen Thursday
and John Wayne as Captain Kirby York in 1948's *Fort Apache*.

from his Civil War rank of general to take command of the Seventh Cavalry. He resents being sent to the desert outpost as much as he resents his demotion; he's arrogant and officious and doesn't understand the tight-knit culture of the men he must lead. He neither understands nor respects the culture of the Apache nation, who are threatening war. He woefully underestimates the strength and power of this enemy, considering them savages without honor, and thus he dooms his company to an ill-conceived and bloody slaughter.

Duke's Kirby York couldn't be more different. He has an easy command of himself and other men. He loves and understands his soldiers, allowing them a certain amount of freedom in dress and deportment, which he feels is appropriate considering the remoteness of the outpost they are duty-bound to protect. Colonel Thursday, on the other hand, is a martinet—despite his objections to the contrary—who insists on West Point spit and polish on all occasions and is ruthless and ignorant in his dealings with the Apaches, unlike Captain York, who knows their chief to be a man of his word. A widower, he ends up derailing his daughter's budding romance with the young second lieutenant Michael "Mickey" Shannon O'Rourke, who is just returning to the fort, where he was raised, after graduating from West Point. Thursday considers O'Rourke beneath him socially, even though the young soldier, like Thursday himself, has West Point credentials. Surprised that a man of low class would be awarded an appointment to the august military academy, Thursday is informed that Mickey's father, Sergeant Major Michael O'Rourke, played by Ward Bond, won the Medal of Honor while serving in New York's Irish Brigade during the Civil War, and thus earned his son's appointment. But that's not good enough. Blinded by class prejudice, Thursday refuses to see Mickey as the soldier and gentleman that he is: a good match for a commander's daughter.

Shirley Temple, whose childhood glory days included Ford's *Wee Willie Winkie*—another film depicting the workings of a military outpost, this one set in India—is a winsome young woman by

1947 and appears as Colonel Thursday's daughter, Philadelphia, who accompanies her stiff-necked father to his new post. She immediately falls in love with Mickey O'Rourke, played by her real-life husband at the time, John Agar. In a reversal of the standard romantic recognition scene, it's the girl who is overwhelmed by her first sight of the boy's beauty. Thursday and his daughter stop at a way station on the road to the cavalry outpost, where they encounter Mickey, also en route to Fort Apache. When they arrive, O'Rourke has stripped down to his trousers to wash up. The sight of the handsome, bare-chested, blond soldier mightily impresses Philadelphia, so when O'Rourke later makes his de rigueur duty call on his new commanding officer, the officer's daughter is already smitten. His youthful but distinctly masculine appearance also delights his fellow soldiers, all of whom he has not seen in some years. Led by Sergeant Festus Mulcahy, played by Victor McLaglen, they have come to escort O'Rourke back to the outpost, whereupon Mulcahy immediately turns the youth over his knee and spanks him, a kind of initiation rite that acknowledges their friendship as well as O'Rourke's new, manly status—as in, this is the last time O'Rourke will ever be spanked. This is but one of numerous scenes with an obvious homoerotic element; in others, Ford's handsome young actors strip down to their bare, smooth chests.

Former John Ford actor George O'Brien returned from movie obscurity in a small but important role as Captain Sam Collingwood, who is retiring from the army but still on the post awaiting a transfer to West Point, where he will become a teacher—a much-desired appointment. He will be the most tragic victim of Thursday's wrongheaded battle with the Apaches, slaughtered just as his new orders have arrived. The athletic O'Brien had been, like Wayne, a former property boy and stuntman at Fox. He had been a boxer and a lifeguard, and he knew how to ride a horse. Described by actress Joanne Dru as "poetic" and "beautiful," he had been cast as the lead in *The Iron Horse*, according to his son, the novelist Darcy O'Brien, because "he demonstrated he was able to pick up a hat off the ground at full gallop." Ford and O'Brien made six more movies together in the 1920s and early 1930s, but in 1947 they had barely spoken during the previous fifteen years, a deep schism caused by an ill-fated trip to the Philippines.

In January 1931, Ford invited O'Brien to accompany him on a trip to the islands, one he'd originally planned to take with his wife, Mary. At the last minute, deciding to rough it and travel by freighter, he essentially gave O'Brien Mary's ticket, and the two men set off on what was to be a grand adventure. Mary reportedly showed up to see the men off at the dock, weeping at being so summarily replaced as a traveling companion. But once they were there, it was a grinding sojourn, including twelve days in the grip of a typhoon, and the two men fell out. Ford grew bored and began drinking heavily; he was disappointed in O'Brien's intellectual capabilities, calling him "Muscles." Ford was a surly drunk, and by February, O'Brien continued the trip to Shanghai alone, leaving Ford to fend for himself.

The rupture badly damaged O'Brien's career. Like Wayne after his setback with Ford, O'Brien found work in B Westerns, but unlike Wayne his life as a leading man was virtually over. In 1947, O'Brien was hurting; his whole career had stalled out. His wife at the time, actress Marguerite Churchill, begged Ford to give O'Brien a part in *Fort Apache*. Ford reportedly answered, "I wouldn't give that son of a bitch a part if he were the last actor on earth after what he did to me in the Philippines." It was only when Marguerite appealed to Ford's Catholicism, which Ford still clung to in spirit if not practice, that he decided to cast O'Brien in the small role of Captain Collingwood.

*

Casting Henry Fonda, longtime hero of Ford's earlier films, as the arrogant and wrongheaded Colonel Thursday, and Duke Wayne as the truly heroic, if conflicted, Captain York, marks an interesting stage in Ford's expression of the American hero. Part of it has to do with sheer physical presence—for John Ford, size mattered. His heroes (and antiheroes) were, increasingly, outsized men with impressive physiques—George O'Brien in *The Iron Horse*, Victor McLaglen in *The Informer*, John Wayne of course, and brawny Ward Bond, often the hero's second-in-command.

Henry Fonda, tall but lean, lacks the burly physique that makes natural-born leaders out of O'Brien, McLaglen, Bond, and Wayne. Fonda is more convincing playing outsiders and loners struggling for a place in the sun—Tom Joad in *The Grapes of Wrath*, a Wyatt Earp who reluctantly takes up the post of sheriff in *My Darling Clementine*, and Abraham Lincoln as a young country lawyer no one expects to achieve great things in *Young Mr. Lincoln*. These characters are complex, somewhat intellectual; they stand at an oblique angle to the world, are forced by circumstances to act and to lead. They embody the reluctant hero model that anchors Ford's earlier films: a man who is nuanced and sometimes skeptical of what he has to do, but as the hero he does it anyway.

After World War II, Ford's idealized hero became less nuanced, less introspective. He moved away from Fonda and increasingly replaced him with John Wayne and his ilk, whose valor and leadership are immediately obvious and who instinctively take command with little or no soul-searching. One film critic likened it to replacing a first wife who had become troublesome with a more pliable second wife; though Wayne's persona was never pliable, the actor himself remained grateful and obedient to John Ford throughout his lifetime.

On *Fort Apache*, Ford bullied and enraged Fonda, to the point of making him cry. "I literally saw tears coming out of Henry Fonda's eyes on *Fort Apache*," recalled Michael Wayne, the actor's son who had accompanied his father to Monument Valley. Years later, Ford would famously break with Fonda when he took over the direction of *Mister Roberts*, bullying the cast Fonda had transported from the drama's long-running Broadway incarnation and causing such strife on the set that Ford ended up punching Fonda in the nose. The two never spoke again.

Another difference between Fonda's Colonel Thursday and the other men at Fort Apache is Thursday's pinched humorlessness. Victor McLaglen's Sergeant Mulcahy especially provides comic relief as a hard-drinking, brawling Irishman who lands in the brig with two cohorts after drinking up the illegal firewater being sold to the Apaches by a nefarious Bureau of Indian Affairs agent. The cavalrymen express their camaraderie with jokes and banter, all of which offends Thursday. But what really marks Thursday as a failed leader is his complete misjudgment of the enemy, the Apache nation.

Captain York, who respects the valor and bravery of Cochise (Miguel Inclan), the great Apache tribal chief, promises his war party safe passage back to the reservation, but Thursday goes against that promise and plans an attack. York is furious that Thursday has made a liar out of him, violating his sense of honor, and he recognizes that the battle Thursday has planned will lead his men into a box canyon where they will be slaughtered. It's a suicide march, and York knows it, but no one can convince Thursday otherwise. Thursday is motivated not just by his low regard of the Apache warriors but by his realization that a victory against Cochise would bring him personal glory, redeeming his demotion to what he considers an ignominious post.

On the cusp of the disastrous battle, unable to change Thursday's mind and blinded by righteous anger, York breaks rank, literally throws down his gauntlet challenging his superior officer to a duel, and is of course immediately ordered to leave the battlefield to be court-martialed. Sending York to the back of the lines, he orders young Mickey O'Rourke to go with him, a tacit acknowledgment that York may be right about the impending slaughter and an effort to keep O'Rourke alive to marry his daughter. If Thursday has had a change of heart about O'Rourke's suitability as a son-in-law, it's only because he's now facing the prospect of his own death, which would leave his daughter orphaned. It's a moment of insight that things will not go his way, but it's too late to change the course of events and still remain the leader he believes himself to be.

The rest is history. All the men are slaughtered, but Thursday makes one last, heroic stand with his men, taking a fatal arrow for one of his soldiers. York witnesses it.

Fast-forward to several years later. York is visited by journalists asking for his comment on a famous painting heroically portraying Thursday's last battle against the Apaches. Was he really the valiant warrior depicted in the painting, which has made Thursday the hero of schoolboys everywhere? York now has his moment of truth: Should he tell them what really happened, or let the falsehood, now legend, stand?

York, who now commands Fort Apache, defends Colonel Thursday's honor. Yes, it was just as it's portrayed in the painting, he lies, and as we see him don the same uniform as his ignoble predecessor, he makes it clear that the legend should be preserved to uphold the honor of the cavalry and the men who will carry on its tradition. The cohesiveness of the cavalry is worth more than the truth. If Captain York was disloyal to Colonel Thursday in life, in death he proves his enduring loyalty both to the institution and to the memory of Thursday's last act of heroism, fighting to the death alongside his doomed men. In York's eyes, that final act has redeemed Thursday's terrible blunder, brought about through ignorance, stubbornness, and pride.

To a contemporary audience, it seems a shocking conclusion. We know the truth, yet here is the film's hero, the character with whom we most identify, perpetuating the lie. By preserving the esprit de corps at the expense of truth, *Fort Apache* eerily foreshadows the Vietnam War roughly fifteen years later, the conflict that made America question itself, that turned generations against each other and against the military, ending the draft. As in *Fort Apache*, the Vietnam War hinged on underestimating and reviling the enemy as savages, less than human, and without honor. Curiously, John Wayne's Captain York takes the position of the man who refuses to fight in a battle he knows is unwinnable because it's based on wrongful contempt for and ignorance of the enemy and the battlefield. In this instance, it's Wayne who's the pacifist!

The audience sides with Wayne's character because his is the side of truth, and yet Ford backs away from that daring refusal to fight a lost cause based on false premises. Instead, he resolves that the purpose and the glory of the military unit are worth more than individual battles, right or wrong. Again *Fort Apache* works as a paradigm for the ill-fated Vietnam War several decades later: those who defended the war often did so by claiming that America's glory and self-image were at stake and that the United States needed to act out of loyalty to its allies, no matter the cost of an unwinnable war. For those in the military, the sacred rule is to always follow the chain of command, to show obedience and respect to the rank, if not the man—in other words, unquestioning loyalty. For those not in the military, blind loyalty is far harder to stomach.

At the end of the battle, Captain York orders Mickey O'Rourke to "go back and marry that girl!" meaning the colonel's daughter. The directive is as much a continuation of the officer's legacy as a sentimental recognition of the couple's love for each other. For Ford, at least in the Cavalry Trilogy's first two films, the importance of marriage lies in its preservation of continuity—especially male continuity—and indeed Philadelphia and Michael have a baby boy at the end of the movie, no doubt headed to West Point one day. Perhaps that's the deeper reason that Thursday ordered York to take Michael safely with him, behind the fray, so he could marry his daughter and produce a male heir, carrying on the military tradition.

Mission accomplished.

＊

Like Alfred Hitchcock, Ford returned to the same themes and milieus throughout his long and productive career, and the value of myth would occupy him again in later films, most famously at the end of *The Man Who Shot Liberty Valance*, when newspaper editor Maxwell Scott actually says, "When the legend becomes fact, print the legend." But does Ford believe that the "legend"—that is, the myth—is more important than the truth? Does it just have to do with storytelling, the basic business of the movies? In Ford's films, to what extreme will men go to protect the legend? Captain York is portrayed as a truth teller with respect for and understanding of the Apaches, but he does the unthinkable: he disobeys orders. Yet he ends up as commander of the outpost, following in Thursday's (wrongfully) hallowed footsteps. For John Ford, Captain York's refusal to loyally follow the disastrous orders of his commanding officer is the right thing to do, but so is remaining loyal to the memory of Colonel Thursday for the sake of the cavalry.

So in *Fort Apache*, it seems Ford wanted it both ways: to recognize York's courage in refusing to fight, and to insist on the importance of maintaining esprit de corps. In real life, that is almost impossible to do. Ford knew that history is replete with myths that crowd out truth. Peter Bogdanovich has noted, "A lot of people thought that in that last scene in *Fort Apache*, Duke was making an apologia for Fonda's character; it wasn't that at all. The conception was that the spirit of the army was more important than the misdirection, or the racism, of one leader. It wasn't an apologia: he's not saying that Fonda was right but that *history* would say that Fonda was right."

This level of subtlety and ambiguity exists throughout *Fort Apache*. On the surface, Ford's is an idealized world of honorable men living, working, and soldiering alongside each other, with their women providing emotional support. Yet the movie is replete with moral ambiguities and subtle hierarchies of power, such as when Ward Bond orders Lieutenant Colonel Thursday out of his house, because within his own home the master of the house has authority over his superior officer. An important nicety for Ford, who, at least in his movies if not in real life, celebrated the sanctity of the home and, more important, gave male societies a certain cozy domesticity.

But after his service in the Field Photographic Branch of World War II, and subsequent decoration as honorary admiral in his beloved navy, Ford's belief in the military became an absolute, replacing his more nuanced view of what it meant to be a hero. His American hero—increasingly embodied by John Wayne—would eventually become an inflexible, tough-minded, solitary man, sacrificing all for patriotism and the cohesiveness of the military.

SHE WORE A YELLOW RIBBON

In *Yellow Ribbon*, the second film in the trilogy, heroic nuance is, thankfully, still in play. There are two tender scenes that belie any attempt to paint the stock Wayne hero as a gun-happy alpha male, one in particular that Ford—a merciless taskmaster but a sentimentalist after all—later said he felt was John Wayne's greatest acting. Late in the film, cavalry post commander Captain Nathan Brittles says farewell to his troops on the day of his retirement and receives a silver watch as a token of their appreciation and respect. Playing a middle-aged man who must fish out his reading glasses to read the inscription on the back of the watch, Wayne brushes away a tear and then blusters his way through the rest of the scene. If nothing else, Ford's admiration for this scene tells us a lot about John Ford.

Then there is the scene where Wayne's Captain Brittles waters the flowers on the grave of his deceased wife, Mary, pouring out his heart to her. It's an unusual scene. Although strong women do emerge in Ford's Cavalry Trilogy, the emotional center of each film is found in the camaraderie of men—soldiers, sons, and commanding officers. Women primarily exist as the worthy objects of soldiers' gallantry or as supportive military wives and daughters, but the important struggles occur among men, and the highest form of loyalty is always to the corps.

In *Fort Apache*, for example, Anna Lee plays Emily Collingwood, Captain Sam Collingwood's wife. She is reluctant to see her husband riding off to one last battle under Colonel Thursday's orders on the eve of his retirement, but she displays the loyalty of a good army wife by insisting it's the choice Collingwood had to make to remain a good soldier—the highest good available to him and to all the men at Fort Apache. Joanne Dru, who co-starred in *She Wore a Yellow Ribbon*, felt that Ford "really didn't relate to women. I've often thought that Papa had tremendous insecurities—never regarding his talent, but as a man. He surrounded himself with these big, strong bruisers. He was an emotional man and a man of many moods."

She Wore a Yellow Ribbon acknowledges the importance of women in the masculine world of the military, albeit in a limited capacity, beginning with the title of the film. "She Wore a Yellow Ribbon" is a marching song used by the military to keep cadence, but it refers to the custom of young women wearing a yellow ribbon in tribute to a sweetheart in the army. Unlike *Fort Apache*, the title shifts focus away from an entirely homosocial setting to one that pays attention to women who would, through marriage, become soldiers' wives, which Ford saw as a great calling.

Few women are "army enough to stay the winter," as the commander's wife, Mrs. Abbey Allshard, played by Mildred Natwick, says about her visiting niece, Olivia Dandridge, played by Joanne Dru, whose insistence at being escorted from Fort Starke to a stagecoach depot brings about a military disaster. Being "army enough to stay the winter" is an admirable trait in Ford's universe; though their character is tested in somewhat different ways, women have to prove their toughness and their worth as much as men do.

In *Yellow Ribbon*, the cavalry is at war with Cheyenne and Arapaho braves who have been stirred up by the defeat of George Armstrong Custer and further encouraged by a mystical sign: the return of buffalo to their hunting grounds. Olivia's presence on a rescue mission has slowed down the cavalry's progress across the desert, so when they arrive at the stagecoach depot, only a few wounded soldiers and terrified women and children are left alive. The slaughter has already taken place, claiming the outpost's commanding officer and his wife. Their mission aborted, the cavalry

*

Duke Wayne as cavalry officer Captain Nathan Brittles
in *She Wore a Yellow Ribbon* in 1949.
This was Ford's favorite performance of Wayne's.

brings the survivors back to headquarters at Fort Starke, doubling up on their horses as they rescue the survivors.

Again, McLaglen plays a heavy-drinking, comic Irishman—Sergeant Quincannon—who is feminized despite his brawn and fighting prowess by his concern and care for the traumatized orphans. He rides back to the fort with a young boy on his horse, taking time to pull on a whiskey flask as he explains that it contains necessary medicine—"tastes awful!" he lies. But the tenderness he shows to the massacre survivor is undercut when McLaglen, back at Fort Starke, gets drunk in the bar and knocks out a small cadre of men sent to haul him to the brig. Ford loved these comic brawls, just as he loved poking fun at the image of the drunken Irishman, who is almost always a sympathetic figure who often rises to heroism.

Sergeant Quincannon is also part of the element that domesticates the masculine milieu of the cavalry, even to the point of referring to his commanding officer, his friend Captain Brittles, with the Irish term of affection "darlin'." Another homey touch is the presence of a lazy dog who lies in the dirt during roll call, confounding McLaglen's attempt at corps discipline.

McLaglen had been a formidable figure in his youth—a boxer who had gone fifteen rounds with Jack Johnson—a tough guy who became a gentle giant and whom Ford used not just for comic relief but, ironically, to embody the calmer, even feminine aspects of the soldier's life. In all three films, McLaglen rescues children imperiled by Indian raids and provides for their comfort. That this sentimental role is taken on by the biggest, toughest, and burliest of Ford's actors is part of the director's genius, revealing his complexity by undercutting, or diluting, his long howl of praise for robust, masculine men. While the insight that men who are confident in their masculinity can be nurturing escaped Ford in the practice of his private life, it may be that McLaglen is Ford's artistic stand-in: a big, tough guy on the outside—still very much a brawler, a drinker, and an Irishman—but a sentimental nurturer within. "My grandfather's macho image was part of his time," Dan

Ford explained. "He was a Hemingway type of guy, a Bogart type of guy. He was a man's man—hard drinking, carousing—and he enjoyed the company of men over women. That's the way men were supposed to be in his day. The people associated with him were the same."

✳

One of the most moving scenes in *She Wore a Yellow Ribbon* occurs when Captain Brittles, who has now retired from the army and feels he can act alone, confronts Pony That Walks, the old chief of the Arapahos—played by John Big Tree, a Seneca—and both men regret the impending war between their nations. "We are too old for war. Old men should stop war," they agree, knowing that their soldiers and braves will not listen to old men. As in *Fort Apache*, we see John Wayne as a peacemaker, with the implication that men who have seen war are cautious about starting wars.

Ford had complicated and complex feelings about Native Americans. They are depicted as mysterious and formidable enemies in *The Iron Horse*, indelibly communicated by the shadow of Indian warriors on horseback thrown against a locomotive. A line of warriors suddenly appearing against the horizon has become a cliché of Westerns, but it was Ford who perfected that ominous shot. In *Stagecoach* they are ruthless marauders, but in the first two films of the Cavalry Trilogy, Ford's Native Americans are capable of both savagery—the slaughter of cavalrymen, women, and children—and a certain nobility, which is found in the tribal chiefs and elders.

His view was softened by the Navajo people in Monument Valley, whom Ford befriended and hired as extras in the films made there. The Navajo nation had been hard hit by the Great Depression and by fierce winters, so when Ford first arrived, they were experiencing starvation conditions. "The Navajo loved it when there was a movie coming," recalled Mike Goulding, who owned the Goulding ranch that housed Ford while on location.

"They'd travel in their wagons from a long way off. They wanted jobs, and they got a big lunch when they worked for Mr. John [Ford]. He always said the Navajo were natural-born actors," and he considered many of them his friends. *Rio Grande*, though somewhat harsher than its two predecessors in depicting the brutality of Indian attacks, acknowledges Native American culture by showing ritual songs and dances, and indeed Ford's significant use of the Navajos of Monument Valley adds authenticity to his depiction of the Indian nations.

MONUMENT VALLEY

"The real star of my Westerns has always been the land," Ford once said, and his feelings for Monument Valley were profound. "When I come back from making a Western on location, I feel a better man for it," said Ford. "I like to get in the desert and smell the fresh clean air. You get up early in the morning and go out on location and work hard all day and then you get home and you go to bed early. It's a great life."

Monument Valley's stark, unrelenting grandeur affected many of the actors and crew as well. John Wayne's young son Michael stayed with his father on location at Goulding's ranch during filming, bunking with the crew and actors. It was crowded and uncomfortable, made worse by Ford's bullying. "That's how he kept people on their toes," Michael Wayne later said. "They didn't know when he was going to snap the trap. That's the way he controlled; I think he was sadistic." Nonetheless, Michael remembers nights in Monument Valley as eerily beautiful, a sentiment shared by many of the actors. The ever-present accordion music of Danny Borzage—a musician and a small-part actor in the John Ford stock company—played a large role in romanticizing the landscape. Music on the set was a technique Ford had used when he made silent films, to help create the mood he needed for his actors.

"Ford would have Danny Borzage play the accordion or someone would sing, maybe with no accompaniment," recalled Michael.

"You'd be sitting out there listening, and there'd be lightning flash-ing. There you were with just a bunch of cowboys and Indians, and far off you'd hear [real] Indians. If somebody was sick, they might be doing a sing." He felt the same way on location for *Rio Grande*, in Moab, Utah. In the evenings, when the hard work was over, Ken Curtis or Maureen O'Hara would often sing. "Here [we] were in the middle of the West," Michael remembered, "with bolts of lightning coming out of the sky, or beautiful cloud formations lit by the moon. It was absolutely fabulous."

But Ford's poor treatment of his actors continued, despite the beauty of a landscape infused with music and transcendent light. Besides browbeating his actors to outperform themselves, and beyond just getting the trains to run on time on a tight budget and tighter shooting schedule, Ford wanted to be more like the men he surrounded himself with. Dobe Carey, who had gone through a tough initiation at Ford's hands, once said,

> Duke used to talk about how much Ford wanted to be one of the guys. There'd be a circle of guys on the set—Ben John-son, John Wayne, some of the stuntmen—and Ford would see them laughing and having a good time, and he'd want to be part of that. But when he'd join them, the fun would stop; everybody would start watching what they said because he was the boss. I felt that he missed the camaraderie, for there was a lot of camaraderie in a John Ford company.

Ben Johnson in particular, who played Sergeant Tyree in *Yel-low Ribbon* and owed his acting career to Ford, felt mistreated by him. He agreed with Carey that "Ford was the type of person who wanted to be part of whatever was going on, and he didn't have the capacity to express himself. . . . I think that was one of the reasons he was so cantankerous around us." Ford's grandson, Dan Ford, thought that his grandfather was "aware of his own sensitivity and almost ashamed of it. He was a very guarded man, but I think he surrounded himself with John Wayne, Ward Bond, and those people because they represented the way he wanted to be." Ben Johnson felt that Ford projected himself into the macho images he created on-screen. "Ford liked to watch me ride a horse. He looked like a sack of walnuts on a horse, but he'd set the camera up and have me ride by. All of those guys were better actors than I was, but I could beat them riding a horse. We did those chases over some pretty rough terrain; you had to be tough to survive."

DIVIDED LOYALTY: *RIO GRANDE*

The third film in what became the Cavalry Trilogy got under way when Herbert J. Yates, head of Republic Pictures, promised Ford he would produce the director's long-held dream project of bringing *The Quiet Man* to the screen—in color and filmed in Ireland—if Ford and Wayne would first make another black-and-white Western for Republic. It was John Wayne who had brought the project to Yates at Republic, the studio where Duke had toiled for so many years making B Westerns. It was a comedown for Ford, but he couldn't interest any other studio in making what seemed like a vanity project about a retired Irish American boxer who returns to his ancestral home and takes a fiery Irish girl as his wife.

For the first time in their careers, Wayne was in a position to help his mentor; Wayne's own box office draw made him a more commercially viable property than the auteur long considered one of Hollywood's greatest and most reliable film directors. In terms of their professional relationship, the tide had begun to turn.

Rio Grande was also significant as the first on-screen pairing of John Wayne—reprising his *Fort Apache* role of an older, more duty-bound Lieutenant Colonel Kirby Yorke—with Maureen O'Hara, who played Kathleen Yorke, his long-estranged wife. Wayne and O'Hara would go on to make four more films together, becoming a legendary on-screen couple, so physically and temperamentally suited to each other that it's hard to recall any other actresses Wayne wooed—and battled—in the movies. Wayne seldom appeared as a romantic hero, but his romantic engagements with O'Hara are iconic. Dobe Carey later said that Wayne loved working with O'Hara because she made and kept "great eye contact" with him, important for Wayne as an actor whose greatest strength, besides physical grace and power, was his emotional reactions to those around him. "I learned to react, not to act," he famously said. Short on technique, he needed that stimulus, and he certainly took to heart Ford's dictum that actors act not with their mouths but with their eyes. Wayne and O'Hara's long thwarted love affair and marriage in *Rio Grande* was a preview of the volatile, passionate romance in their next film together, *The Quiet Man*. In the Dublin-born Maureen O'Hara, John Wayne had met his match.

O'Hara—a robust, beautiful woman with flaming hair and green eyes—was tall, sturdy, and strong, commanding enough to pair with John Wayne. And with her tough Irish temperament—and temper—she could stand up to anyone. Cast and crew called her "Big Red." She would remain Wayne's favorite leading actress throughout his life; he once called her "the greatest guy I ever knew."

In *Rio Grande*, John Wayne's most memorable scenes are with O'Hara, when Kirby Yorke is not speaking but reacting to the mood of the scene and to the beautiful Kathleen. In one such scene, the Western singing group the Sons of the Pioneers serenade the couple, who have come together after fifteen years of estrangement. While Ken Curtis sings a love song titled "I'll Take You Home Again, Kathleen" in his beautiful baritone, no words are exchanged between Yorke and Kathleen, yet the pull of fifteen years of loneliness and Wayne's unabated love for the formidable woman at his side are palpable. This is John Wayne as a great film actor, conveying deep but conflicting emotions with his eyes and his posture. Yorke would make the same choice again—fidelity to duty over wife and son—if he had to. But it would pain him mightily. Understanding this, Kathleen says bitterly, "What makes soldiers great is hateful to me."

✳

Duke Wayne and his favorite co-star, Maureen O'Hara,
in *Rio Grande*, 1950. "She's the greatest guy I ever knew," he once said
of the Irish actress.

We learn that Kathleen, a southerner, has already lost her ancestral home, the plantation Bridesdale, which was burned down by order of General Sheridan. Her own husband carried out those orders, and the "arsonist" Quincannon lit the house personally. (The incident is based on the alleged burning of the ancestral home of Ford's wife.) It's another reason for their estranged marriage—York's sense of duty to his commanding officer trumping fealty to his wife. Having lost so much, Kathleen now fears she will lose her son down the same path that claimed her husband. But we know that her ministrations and her attempt to force her son to leave the cavalry would humiliate him. So husband and wife, brought briefly together, are irrevocably divided.

When Wayne tries to explain, "I've seen things that make my sense of duty important," she answers, "I'm sorry your sense of duty destroyed two beautiful things—Bridesdale and us." And later, "My only rival is the U.S. Cavalry." Because she is so strong a presence and so commanding as an actress, Ford manages to balance the agonizing pull between duty and love.

Ford, too, was smitten with Maureen O'Hara. They had a strong connection due to their Irish heritage, and in fact Ford delighted in speaking some limited Gaelic with her on the set of *The Quiet Man*. But as he often did, Ford expressed his admiration—perhaps even love—through cruelty, which extended beyond the movie set. In her memoir *'Tis Herself*, O'Hara describes a harrowing incident that took place at one of John and Mary Ford's parties in December 1944 at the director's home.

"The usual gang was there," she wrote, "and after mingling with the guests downstairs for a bit, I went upstairs and found Pappy on a chaise longue in the middle of telling a story to some friends." She slipped into the room and took a seat next to him as he recounted one of "his favorite lies" about riding with Pancho Villa. When one of the guests asked O'Hara a question and she answered, suddenly Ford turned on her and socked her in the jaw. "I felt my head snap back and heard the gasps of everyone there as each of them stared at me in disbelief and shock. I don't know why he hit me, and to this day, I still don't have a clue."

In a 2012 interview, the actress, then ninety-two and still strong and clear-minded, repeated the refrain oft sung about the irascible Ford—that he was brutal but somehow it was all worth it:

> There were times when you wanted to die because he could be so tough and so cruel and so mean. He was mean to everybody! Not just John Wayne. He was with me, with Harry Carey [Jr.]. And they all said to Ford, "Yes, sir, yes, sir! Where? Now?" And yet when you did something good, and he told you it was good, why, you were floating up the sky! You'd want to kill him, and five minutes later you could've thanked him or hugged him . . . because you knew your day's work was good.

Though he considered *Rio Grande* "a throwaway" to satisfy the demands of Republic Pictures, Ford knew it still had to be good. Some film critics consider it the weakest of the trilogy, but in retrospect it may be the most beautiful and most compelling. This time Ford filmed in Moab, Utah, in a landscape that Dobe Carey described as "a miniature Monument Valley—the monuments are just smaller." Ford had filmed in Moab earlier that year when he made *Wagon Master*, about a wagon train of Mormons making their perilous way westward, so he knew how well it could suit his needs. The Colorado River ran through the area, which doubled as the Rio Grande bordering Mexico—Río Bravo to the Mexicans—which the U.S. Cavalry is forbidden to cross even in pursuit of marauding Apaches who have been conducting raids across the river. J. Carrol Naish plays Lieutenant General Philip Sheridan, and he reminds Yorke that "soldiers don't make policy" when Yorke wants to illegally cross into Mexico to root out the Apaches. Both men know it's against orders, and both chafe at that, but—for a time—they bow to it.

The opening of the film is stirring. We see exhausted cavalry-men returning after an engagement with the Apaches from the point of view of women and children living on the cavalry outpost. There is no dialogue, just a silent search along the line for return-ing husbands and fathers. This is what it meant, to Ford, to be a military wife—to wait, to support, to search among faces for the loved one's return. As a silent film director, he knew the power of the camera without words, and it sets the tone of sacrifice and hardship among the cavalrymen and their women. It's an arche-typal scene, reminiscent of the ragtag women following Foreign Legion soldiers at the beginning and ending of the 1930 Marlene Dietrich–Gary Cooper movie, *Morocco*.

While the opening is indeed a somber one, this would not be a Ford Western if it didn't also have broad comedy, and again the reliable Victor McLaglen provides it, reprising his role of Quincan-non. By way of explaining this recurring character, Ford said, "A lot of the Irish went west after the Civil War; I'm quite enthused about [this] as a bit of Americana." Though McLaglen began his career with Ford in *The Informer*, a decidedly non-comedic role, his transformation from tragedy to comedy was complete by the time he appeared in the Cavalry Trilogy.

In the intervening years since the setting of *Fort Apache*, Kirby Yorke, the top commander of the fort, has taken on some of the qualities of the hard-liner Colonel Thursday. His sixteen-year-old son, Jefferson, played by Claude Jarman Jr., has just flunked out of West Point and enlisted in the cavalry, and Yorke tells him to expect not glory in the military but hardship, suffering, and "fidel-ity to duty." He will not even publicly acknowledge that Jeff is his son, in part because they have been estranged for most of the boy's life.

Though Yorke will not sign the papers allowing Kathleen to buy Jefferson out of the cavalry because the boy "needs to learn to stand by his word," he defers to her by having his son accompany the women and children to Fort Bliss, out of harm's way. "You hate it, but I love you for it," Kathleen says. Ironically, the Apaches attack this supposedly safe passage, and it is Ben Johnson—as Trooper Travis Tyree—who saves the day.

Ben Johnson is considered by many the best stuntman to ever act in pictures; he doubled Fonda in *Fort Apache,* and his ease and beauty on a horse, particularly in *She Wore a Yellow Ribbon,* is poetry in motion. He often downplayed his abilities as an actor, but he's winning in *Rio Grande* as a young Texan on the lam from a manslaughter charge, hoping to hide out in "this man's army."

This was Ben Johnson's third role as a credited actor rather than a stuntman. He had grown up in Oklahoma and was a rodeo star before working in the film industry. "I've been able to ride a horse ever since I could walk," he once said. "It's second nature to me. Riding is like dancing; it's all timing." His charisma on-screen was also natural, and the combination of abilities would serve him well. Twenty-one years later, Peter Bogdanovich—who worshipped Ford—would cast Ben Johnson in *The Last Picture Show,* in homage to Ford as much as in recognition of Ben Johnson's abilities as a fine actor as well as a horseman.

In *Rio Grande,* Johnson's skills are proven in his first scene, when Sergeant Quincannon challenges his new cavalry recruits to ride "Roman style." Tyree immediately leaps across the backs of two horses, grabs the reins, and stands upright astride the two racing beasts. He magnificently jumps a fence in this stance, a breathtaking feat. Dobe Carey then follows suit. Both men admitted that it took them three weeks to master the stunt, though each had grown up riding horses. Meanwhile, Jarman mastered the feat almost immediately, which Ben Johnson put down to his being too young to know how dangerous the stunt was.

In another particularly daring scene, Tyree escapes from three Apaches in hot pursuit by pulling his horse to the ground and using the animal as a shield. It's not just any horse, but Colonel Yorke's, which Tyree has stolen in an attempt to escape from the U.S. marshal intent on dragging him back to Texas to stand trial. It's an amazing stunt—reprised, incidentally, in Larry McMurtry's epic *Lonesome Dove.*

Ben Johnson credits Ford with educating him in the motion picture business, but he didn't come around to worshipping Ford for his ability to force or humiliate his actors into giving their best performances. It may be because Johnson didn't start out to be an actor, nor did he consider it his main calling; he was as good as he needed to be, and his greatest contribution was his brilliant stunt work, which few others could provide. He had nothing to prove. Like McLaglen, who had won an Academy Award in Ford's *Informer* and had been a heavyweight boxer, Johnson was secure in his masculinity and his abilities. He stood up to Ford's bullying, but he long resented him for it.

An unfortunate incident while making *Rio Grande* would herald thirteen long years before the actor ever worked with John Ford again. At dinner one night, Ford took offense at a joke that John Wayne made, but he mistakenly called Ben Johnson out for it. "Hey, stupid," he yelled, and demanded that Ben repeat the joke. Ben got up and said to Ford, "Well, you can just shit in your hat." He stomped out of the mess hall and did not return that night. Ford turned to Dobe Carey, telling him, "Oh, Jesus Christ, Dobe, go get him, for God's sake, and bring him back."

Dobe recalled, "He knew he'd been wrong. He'd made a mistake and let his temper and vanity overcome him." Ford had banished George O'Brien and Harry Carey for murkier reasons. Ford would get mad at his actors and not use them "for long periods of time, to punish them for whatever he thought they had done wrong. He did that all his motion-picture life, starting with my dad [Harry Carey] in 1921. And any little thing could trigger it and get you on his 'you're a bad boy' list." Dobe himself would become a target for Ford's temper after breaking one of Ford's strictest commandments: no alcohol for the duration of a film shoot.

Joanne Dru, who played Olivia Dandridge in *She Wore a Yellow Ribbon*, recalled that "Ford loved drunks. Who of that bunch wasn't an alcoholic? If you didn't drink, he looked at you with a jaundiced eye, but not during a picture. When the picture was over, you could go to his house and stumble all over the place and

﹡

Ben Johnson, the great horseman and character actor
in 1949's *She Wore a Yellow Ribbon*. He clashed badly with
Ford during the making of *Rio Grande*.

he didn't care." Perhaps that was why Ford constantly chewed on a handkerchief during those long, dry location shoots. "He's always eatin' on a handkerchief," Ben Johnson said, probably to keep himself from drinking while satisfying an oral compulsion. He would throw anyone off the set if he smelled alcohol on his or her breath.

Years later, Ford broke one of Dobe Carey's ribs while filming a comic fight scene in *Two Rode Together*, starring James Stewart and Richard Widmark. Dobe and Dick Widmark had been out drinking until dawn—they'd each polished off four double margaritas in one particular Mexican establishment—and though Widmark, who usually didn't drink, seemed unscathed, Dobe showed up on location decidedly the worse for wear.

Ford showed no mercy in the staged fight, usually choreographed to avoid injury, but this time the director yelled, "All right, go at it! Make it goddamned rough. Action!" After a few takes, Dobe was exhausted, suffering from heat exhaustion. Dobe recalled,

> Between one of the takes, Uncle Jack came over to the three of us while we were lying on the ground. I was lying on my stomach, head-to-toe beside Dick [Widmark], trying to catch my breath. Uncle Jack . . . came up beside me and fell to his knees. One knee buried itself in my back between my ribs. He leaned as hard as he could on that knee while he reached over and fiddled with Dick's neckerchief. Then I heard a sound like a dry stick of wood breaking in half.
>
> Andy Devine, who was a considerable distance away, said, "There goes Dobe's ribs!"

SONS OF THE PIONEERS

Rio Grande is more visually stirring than the other two trilogy Westerns, with stunning vignettes: Wayne walking along the Colorado River, his weathered, pained face juxtaposed against the majestic landscape, while the Sons of the Pioneers sing their songs. Wayne has never looked as strong and iconic as he does in *Rio Grande*. Strong men are moved by music, Ford shows us, as we see in the faces of Yorke and Sheridan and Quincannon listening to Ken Curtis's serenades.

Ford loved the sound of male voices singing in harmony, and he used male choruses in many of his films. Ford welcomed Curtis into the family when he married Ford's daughter, Barbara, with the sly comment that now he could hear his favorite songs sung at any time. The use of Americana music, even if sometimes anachronistic, served both to create an ambience and to reflect the historical fact that Civil War soldiers on both sides sang to lift their spirits. There was so much suffering on the battlefield that singing was one of the few soldier's joys.

The Sons of the Pioneers, led by the versatile Curtis, provided the almost continuous music for *Rio Grande*—love songs like "I'll Take You Home Again, Kathleen," marching songs like "Footsore Cavalry," cowboy ballads like "Cattle Call," and working songs like "Low Bridge (Fifteen Miles on the Erie Canal)." Strains of "Dixie" are played at the film's end, suitable considering the film is set just at the end of the Civil War. Closing with this classic southern tune demonstrates that the tensions between troops from the North and the South, very much present at the outset, are resolved by the end of the movie, just as the split between Lieutenant Colonel Yorke and Kathleen moves ultimately toward a kind of reconciliation, a resolution effected in no small part by their son's actions.

Throughout the picture, the recruits are all addressed as "boy," and to underline that status early in the film, Yorke's very boyish-looking son, Jeff, gets into a fistfight with a soldier who is much older, bigger, and more muscular—almost a caricature of a tough, full-grown man. We see the vast gulf Jeff has to bridge before he can be called a man, and when his commanding officer and father, Yorke, arrives on the scene of the brutal, uneven fight, he allows it to continue as a lesson to his son. It's not important who wins the fight; what's important is the younger boy's willingness to engage and to defend himself. Of course, the older, heavier soldier dominates, but when the fight is over, Quincannon—the oldest and biggest one of all—punches him out.

On one hand, this is a lesson in survival, but it's also a demonstration that to achieve maturity, the boy has to take on the man. Between Roman riding and no-holds-barred fisticuffs, it's not clear that Jefferson Yorke will survive this man's army. However, the boy proves his worth by helping to rescue the children kidnapped by the Apaches. And when his father is grievously wounded in the attack, he asks his son to pull out the Apache's arrow. It's a feat that takes physical strength and an unflinching ability to inflict pain on a loved one in order to save his life—the very lesson Yorke has been trying to teach his son all along.

The movie ends as it began, with exhausted and wounded soldiers trailing back to the fort, but now it is only Kathleen we see, scouring their faces to see if her husband is among them. When she sees him being transported back on a pallet, she takes his hand, and Yorke tells Kathleen, "Our boy did well," hinting that the two may finally be reunited in their marriage.

SOLDIER'S CAUSE

Over the course of the Cavalry Trilogy, women take on roles of greater significance, from Shirley Temple's Philadelphia to Maureen O'Hara's Kathleen, who is far more Wayne's equal than a helpless dependent. But Joanne Dru, as Olivia Dandridge, is more problematical. She isn't tough enough to "stay the winter," which means she would not make a good army wife, and she puts the troops in peril when she needs to be rescued. The trailer for *She Wore a Yellow Ribbon* says it all: "Because of her, men fight heroically. Because of her, men die."

The woman has to be worthy of gallantry and protection—and only sometimes of desire, because Ford was not comfortable filming love scenes, which he considered going against "my nature, my religion, and my natural inclinations." When she is not—when she has been unfaithful, tarnished, or otherwise deemed unworthy of male sacrifice and bravery, then the urge to protect turns into the urge to destroy. This is what we see in Ford's greatest Western, *The Searchers.*

4

The Avenging Loner: The Searchers

Don't let the boys waste their lives in vengeance.
—SPOKEN BY MRS. JORGENSEN IN *THE SEARCHERS*

I didn't know that the big son of a bitch could act.
—JOHN FORD

The *Searchers* is John Ford's masterpiece. In 2007, the American Film Institute (AFI) ranked it twelfth in its list of the best hundred movies; the following year, the AFI deemed it the greatest Western ever made. Released in 1956, it was John Ford's 115th film, his 12th made with John Wayne, and his 5th picture shot in Monument Valley. Film director Curtis Hanson, who made *L.A. Confidential,* among other films, has described this particular John Ford and John Wayne partnership as one of film history's great collaborations. The film exposes America's deeply embedded racism through John Wayne's role as the vengeful Ethan Edwards. Revenge is a central motivating aspect of this role for Wayne, different in many ways from the hero he was by then well loved for playing. In fact it signaled a shift from his more traditional heroes to the grizzled persona that Wayne came to embody in many of the thirty-seven feature films that followed. But it wasn't the first such character he played: Wayne's role in Howard Hawks's 1948 film *Red River* gave us our first glimpse of Duke Wayne as a hardened, take-no-prisoners patriarch, tougher than the characters he plays in Ford's Cavalry Trilogy.

In *Red River,* Duke plays Tom Dunson, a rancher driven to near madness by the difficulties in herding ten thousand head of cattle from Texas to Missouri. He lashes out against his adopted son, Matthew Garth, played by Montgomery Clift, when Matthew rightfully takes the cattle away from him and diverts the herd to Abilene, Kansas. Dunson begins as a "good" man, but he is increasingly crazed by a growing awareness of his impossible journey, by his lack of sleep, and by the defection of some of his drovers, whom he's threatened to lynch for abandoning the cattle drive and stealing rations. He becomes tyrannical, unable to admit that he's been wrong on insisting that they head for Missouri instead of Abilene, a more direct, though untried, route, and unable to accept any challenges to his authority, especially from Matt.

Red River's romantic subplot features Joanne Dru as the feisty Tess Millay, a dance hall girl traveling with a gambling outfit and bordello heading to Las Vegas, though she insists that she's "not one of them"—that is, not a prostitute. After catching Matt's attention, she brings the warring father and son together by angrily reminding them that they do indeed love each other. It's a scene dictated by rigid cultural convention, the late 1940s and the 1950s idea of women as emotionally astute but living only to make the lives of their men easier.

When Hawks uses immigrants and nonwhite characters, such as a stock Irishman and a comic Indian sidekick, it's merely to add flavor. Absent is Ford's profound dedication to presenting the expansionist history of America and the nation's melting pot character—the Irish, the Chinese, the Welsh, the Swedes, and the many other ethnic groups who came and often fought together to make the land theirs. Also absent is Ford's willingness to acknowledge that this expansion came at the cost of the Native American way of life—a fact Ford increasingly saw not only from the Anglos' point of view but from the Indians' as well. In *The Searchers*, the Comanche raiding party is shown as savage, but the scene of a smoking Indian village ravaged by the U.S. Cavalry attempts to balance the equation.

This was Wayne's first major role as a vengeful antihero, and it made John Ford reconsider his protégé's range as an actor. In *Red River*, John Wayne is completely convincing in the role of single-minded avenger—a fact that was not lost on Ford. "I didn't know that the big son-of-a-bitch could act," he reportedly said after seeing Hawks's film, and he subsequently cast Wayne as the older Captain Brittles in *She Wore a Yellow Ribbon*, aging him with gray hair and reading glasses. On the occasions admirers thought that *Red River* was a John Ford film, he took the compliment gracefully and didn't correct their error. *Red River* does seem Fordian in visual style, mood, and content, and it was made by a director Ford admired; Hawks greatly admired and looked up to Ford in return. Indeed, Hawks employs elements pioneered by the older director: sweeping western landscapes under roiling skies, a focus on masculine camaraderie as well as disruption among ranks, and few women, but strong, outspoken ones, willing to fight for their man. It's worth noting that Ford's influence was not confined to Hawks's vision for the film; Ford actually worked on the project in a small way, overseeing some of the editing. But *Red River*, though a powerful and enjoyable picture, is less profound than Ford's *Searchers*, which investigates the darkness at the heart of America's western expansion. And Ford would never have resolved a conflict with a speech, as Hawks does; Ford's preference was always for strong visual language, for showing rather than telling.

What is most powerful in *Red River*—besides the beautiful, restrained acting of Monty Clift in his screen debut—is the image of John Wayne as Thomas Dunson stalking Matt with intent to kill. The final scene is merciless: Dunson arrives in Abilene and strides relentlessly through a crush of milling cattle, pushing them out of his way in order to confront his adopted son. The fact that he will not be assuaged—the inevitability of his vengeance—is terrifying. He has gone from hero to villain over the course of the movie, and the audience indeed fears that he will kill Matt. There is an Old Testament quality to Dunson's rage.

This is new territory for John Wayne, whose roles to this point involve increasingly tough characters but not a willingness to kill a loved one. Peter Bogdanovich observes that it took Hawks to discover "the most iconic way for Duke to behave. He could have remained a very likable leading man, but not an icon. Hawks was extraordinary in finding a niche in which the star was most attractive. The same thing with Bogart—he found the quintessential Humphrey Bogart" in *To Have and Have Not*—"and the same thing with Cary Grant, in *Only Angels Have Wings* and *His Girl Friday:* two sides of the same coin."

Ford was irritated that Hawks saw this dimension to Duke before he did, just as he had been angry at Raoul Walsh for poaching his protégé and being the one to give him his new name. But he respected Hawks nonetheless, and the two men remained friends. Hawks, for his part, "had enormous respect for Ford," says Bogdanovich. "In fact, when he was around him, he seemed like a kid around the school headmaster."

Monty Clift makes for a fascinating on-screen combination with the older John Wayne. Clift was a product of the newly influential Method technique by way of Lee Strasberg's famed Actors Studio in New York, while Duke Wayne, B Westerns veteran, cobbled together his approach by absorbing the techniques—or at least the confidence—of his more polished co-stars while under Ford's tyranny. And yet they mesh beautifully, with both actors giving riveting performances. By now Wayne's sheer size and bulk, and the lines on his roughened but still handsome face, give him an authority that contrasts with Clift's youthful, unlined prettiness. In a way, it's an ushering in of Method acting, which would come to dominate in the next few decades, but in this film both styles deliver the same punch. As Martin Scorsese has noted, John Wayne "was always underrated as an actor," but *Red River* shows us the dark depths of his range.

The Searchers would sear those depths into cultural memory.

VENGEANCE IS MINE

The insatiable vengeance possessing Tom Dunson is taken even further in the role of the relentless Ethan Edwards. In *The Searchers*, Ethan enters the picture as a man motivated by his racial hatred of Indians, which is only deepened when a Comanche raiding party slaughters his brother, Aaron; his beloved sister-in-law, Martha, and her son; and kidnaps their two daughters, teenage Lucy and six-year-old Debbie. Ethan joins a posse of deputized Texas Rangers rounded up by Ranger captain the Reverend Samuel Johnson Clayton, played by Ward Bond, and they set out to find the kidnapped girls. Lucy, a young woman, is found raped and murdered by her captors, but of Debbie there is no sign. What follows is the seven-year search to rescue her, carried out by Ethan and his nephew, a handsome youth named Martin Pawley, played by Jeffrey Hunter. Ethan had rescued Martin as an infant after his family was killed by Indians, and Aaron and Martha took the baby in to raise as their own. Though adopted, Martin is very much a part of their family, and he considers Debbie his true sister; he wants nothing but to find her and secure her safety and freedom. As far as he's concerned, she is the only family he has left.

Visually, the film is extraordinarily beautiful, beginning with the now famous opening shot of a western expanse—the red formations of Monument Valley—framed by the threshold of a homestead's dark interior, and a prairie wife, Martha, looking out as Ethan Edwards approaches on horseback. Though the film and the book it was based on—Alan Le May's *The Searchers*—are both set in the flats of West Texas, Ford shot in his beloved Monument Valley. His vistas are clearly inspired by the paintings and pho-

✳

Duke Wayne as the implacable racist Ethan Edwards
in *The Searchers*, 1956. His most terrifying role, and one of his
greatest performances.

tographs of western artists Frederic Remington and Charles M. Russell, particularly in his depictions of Indian camps. His love of horses is expressed here as well, in lyrical but gratuitous shots of the animals swimming and cavorting in rivers, all adding to the painterly grace of Ford's sweeping vistas. Indeed, Scorsese calls *The Searchers* "one of the most beautiful films ever made."

In that opening shot, the cabin's interior is dark against the bright beauty of the landscape, and the waiting woman is reminiscent of the cavalry wives stoically waiting for their husbands to return from their battle with renegade Indians in *Rio Grande*. Historically, Ford shows, men fight, and women wait. The shot of the landscape framed by the cabin's threshold is haunting, and it is also reminiscent of a powerful threshold image in Michael Powell and Emeric Pressburger's 1945 film, *I Know Where I'm Going!*, in which a self-possessed young woman bent on marrying a wealthy industrialist is seen framed in the doorway of a Scottish country house where she will stay the night on her journey to meet her fiancé. She pauses at the threshold and, by entering, entirely changes her fate. This doesn't take away from Ford's originality, because he certainly learned from other directors, such as his atmospheric use of fog and mist in *The Informer*, inspired by F. W. Murnau. Like most great artists, Ford was an avid learner who took what he needed.

But the threshold image is used differently in *The Searchers*. Ford underlines a fundamental conflict in the heart of his hero, and in his own heart as well: the deep pull of domestic, familial, and community places, versus the call of the windswept frontier, beyond the blessings of civilization—the yin and the yang of femininity and masculinity, two realms Ford celebrated and struggled to reconcile in his personal life.

Not to say that women haven't also felt this pull between hearth and horizon—indeed, that yearning helped drive the second wave of feminism—but in Ford Westerns it's the hero who is torn, while female characters express their strength and individuality in other ways. Usually they fight to maintain the integrity of the home, threatened not just by external events but by their men's restless longings, ambitions, or sense of duty, dramatized later in *The Searchers* when Martin sets out on the long search with Ethan to find his captive niece. Martin's fiancée, Laurie Jorgensen, played by Vera Miles, is furious about being left to wither on the vine. "I wasn't cut out to be no old maid!" she wails. She bosses him, she kisses him, she fights with him, she makes it clear that she loves him and that she is his equal, but she finally gives in to his need to follow Ethan on his heroic quest, even giving him her own horse—angrily, reluctantly—to continue the pursuit. One can easily imagine her joining the search in a modern-day, revisionist Western.

Once Ethan crosses the threshold to his brother's homestead, he has entered a domestic haven. The whitewashed adobe brick of the interior glows in the light of the blazing hearth fire; the family gathers along a plank table, joined by their adoptive son, Martin. It's a scene reminiscent of *How Green Was My Valley*, in which family share food with warmth, affection, and some good-natured bickering. But Ethan's racism darkens this version of the domestic scene when he accuses Martin of looking like a half-breed, only to be reminded that he's just part Cherokee, the rest English and Welsh.

Strong emotions pass between Martha and Ethan: he greets her with a kiss on the forehead, a kiss of palpable tenderness. Later she strokes his jacket when she thinks no one can see her. Aaron, Ethan's brother, appears oblivious to these moments, but all kinds of questions are raised by their undeclared love. Talk among the characters reveals that Ethan left to fight for the Confederacy but stayed away three additional years after the surrender, which he still refuses to acknowledge. Did he stay away because he loves his brother's wife? Ethan's unspoken love for Martha, who seems to return it, isn't lost on at least one member of the family. Martha's young son says on the eve of the Comanche attack, "I wish Uncle Ethan was here, don't you, Ma?" And Reverend Clayton notices what passes between them, but pretends not to.

THE URGE TO PROTECT

Many men seem hardwired to protect, and John Wayne often portrayed exactly that type of man. War films are replete with men who risk their lives to save others, and contemporary films such as Liam Neeson's *Taken* franchise rely on just such an imperative—even in an era that offers a wider array of male role models and women who do not want or need male protection, who frankly chafe at the idea.

Ethan Edwards, like Dunson and most heroes of American action movies of the last century, is motivated by an almost blind need to *protect* something—a woman, a family, children, a place—even if he has no apparent claim to it. When Ethan realizes that the party he joined to track down a rancher's stolen bull was intentionally lured away by the Comanches, he quickly heads back to Aaron and Martha's homestead, dreading what he'll find there. He knows he's been tricked, and when he arrives, he finds the cabin burned to the ground. He calls out, "Martha, Martha!" desperate to find her alive, but finds her defiled body in a shed behind the smoldering ruins. Martha's slaughtered body is never actually shown on film. Instead, we see Ethan stumble out of the dark depths of the shed, furious and heartbroken. When Martin comes looking for his aunt Martha, Ethan strikes him, barring his entrance into the killing ground. Later, when he finds Lucy's defiled body, Ethan also refuses to describe what he's seen to her young suitor, Brad Jorgensen, played by Harry Carey Jr. "Don't ever ask me as long as you live," he snarls. Ford knew that his audience could imagine the death and destruction far more graphically than he could ever depict it on-screen. Because it was 1956, depictions of graphic sex and violence were restrained by the Motion Picture Code, but Ford wouldn't have used them even if he could; they weren't part of his aesthetic.

Ethan's love for Martha is part of what motivates his seven-year search, and finding her defiled body after the Comanche raid propels him to action. He wants to avenge her horrific death as much as he wants to find Martha's younger daughter. When that urge to protect—to "safeguard the perimeter"—is thwarted, or refused, or proves unattainable, the hero lashes out in other directions. In *The Searchers*, Ethan's outward anger is directed toward "the Comanche"—spoken derisively in two instead of three syllables, harsh emphasis on the second—but there must also be unspoken anger toward himself for failing to protect the woman he loved and her children, including one who might possibly have been his own. Given his affection toward Debbie at the beginning of the film—he gives her his Civil War medal of honor—it's fair to wonder if Debbie was actually fathered by Ethan, which would partly explain his single-minded quest to find her. And while on the search, he angrily disputes that Debbie is Martin's sister but doesn't elaborate further.

Tom Dunson in *Red River* also failed to protect the "one woman he loved." When the film opens, he's leaving behind his sweetheart, Fen, played by Colleen Gray, so he can strike out on his own in search of land to start his cattle ranch. She sweetly insists on accompanying him, but believing she will be safer with the wagon train, Dunson refuses to allow it. In parting, he gives her a prized bracelet that had belonged to his mother, a token of his love and emblem of his promise to send for her when he secures land. In a cruel irony, she is slaughtered when the wagon train is attacked by Indians, and Dunson and his sidekick, Groot Nadine, played by Walter Brennan, are spared—they're already far away. Heartbroken and guilty, Dunson takes in the only survivor of the massacre, young Matthew, who becomes not only a surrogate son but a kind of surrogate wife. He gives the boy the bracelet that he'd first given to Fen, found on the body of one of the marauding Indian braves. And he mates his bull with the boy's rescued cow, which will be the start of his cattle herd.

Matthew's romantic attraction to Tess, however, softens any hint of mutual attraction between the two men. Even Dunson gets into the act when he meets Tess and guesses her attachment to Matthew. He offers her half of his ranch if she'll bear him a son, in a vengeful attempt to disinherit Matthew and steal his girl. She briefly considers it, if only to save Matt from Dunson's murderous intent.

But Dunson is haunted by his memory of his abandonment of Fen and his failure to protect her. That abandonment is replayed, in a fashion, when Matt appears to abandon Tess to drive the cattle herd to Abilene, ordering her to stay with the wagon train, just as Dunson had done years earlier. When the conflict is finally resolved, Dunson echoes Captain York in *Fort Apache* when he tells Matt to "marry that girl," to keep Matt from repeating his own irrevocable mistake.

※

Halfway through *The Searchers*, when years have gone by in the fruitless pursuit of Debbie, Ethan reveals he is increasingly driven by the desire not just to find the girl but to kill her. He believes that she's been contaminated by life with the Comanches and presumes that she has been taken as the wife of his nemesis, the Comanche warrior known as Scar, played by the German actor Henry Brandon, or by one of his braves. The fact that she's "been living with a buck," in Ethan's words, condemns her to death in his mind, and in the prevailing ethos of the day.

When Martin realizes Ethan's new intention, he devotes his efforts to stopping him. Throughout, Ethan heaps scorn on Martin, calling him "blanket head" and sneering at his mixed-blood heritage. In Ethan's mind, this racial legacy prevents Martin from being a true man, despite partnering up with Ethan, who would otherwise have much to teach him. Ethan repeatedly reminds him that Martin is no blood kin to Debbie or to himself, even as Martin carries on, firm in his conviction to see the quest completed.

Ford, whether intentionally or not, tapped into one of the great conundrums of a traditional masculine impulse: when men fail to protect those they love, or they discover or decide that the ones they're protecting are not worthy of their efforts, those men turn deadly. And often they set out to destroy the very loved ones they had failed to protect in the first place. So Ethan, a hard man who failed to protect the woman he loved and her family, seeks to find and murder the last of her children. It's possible that he not only is carrying out what would now be called an "honor killing" but is perhaps seeking to expunge the last reminder of his failure to protect her and her mother. There are true tales of this behavior: men who murder their families when they can no longer support—and thus protect—them.

On another level, the impulse to murder Debbie is Ethan's way of saving her from what he considers a hellish life, an opinion strengthened by a visit to a U.S. Cavalry fort to find out if one of three white girls rescued from Indian captivity might be Debbie. The encounter makes for a chilling sight; the three former captives are clearly insane. The oldest one, a young woman, maniacally clutches Debbie's doll when Ethan shows it to her. One of the younger girls giggles and stares eerily into space, while the third clings to her as if to life itself. It's an unsettling portrait of the aftermath of captivity—quite different from the true story of Cynthia Ann Parker upon which the novel was based—and it deepens Ethan's lust for revenge. "It's hard to believe they're white," says the cavalry commander who has rescued them, and Ethan answers, "They ain't white, they're Comanche," spitting out the final word. Ford closes in on Ethan's face as he leaves the scene, registering a look of so much hatred, disgust, and resolve that Scorsese has described it as one of the most powerful close-ups in film history.

Alan Le May's novel *The Searchers* is a fictionalized retelling of nine-year-old Cynthia Ann Parker's 1836 abduction by the Comanches in West Texas, and the efforts of the Texas Rangers to find and rescue her. It's a classic captivity narrative, part of a popular genre in eighteenth- and nineteenth-century American fiction centered on white women and children captured by Indians and raised in their culture. Many women and children were indeed captured during the long, bloody skirmishes between Plains Indians and settlers pushing westward, and these novels underlined the pervasive fear of tribal Indians on the frontier. Their depictions of Native savagery helped to justify, in white settlers' minds, the forceful annexation of Indian lands.

But captives often assimilated into Native American cultures, adopting their ways, as Cynthia Ann Parker did. Renamed "Nadua" or "Nauta" by the Comanches, which means "found one" or even more tellingly "one who keeps warm with us," Cynthia lived with a tribe for twenty-four years, marrying the chieftain, Peta Nocona, and bearing him a daughter and two sons. So complete was her assimilation that when she was finally recaptured by the Texas Rangers, she could not integrate back into white society. She died of influenza shortly thereafter, mourning the loss of her Comanche sons. A chronicler of her tale wrote in 1909, "I am convinced that the white people did more harm by keeping her away from them than the Indians did by taking her away in the first place."

While the scene in *The Searchers* showing three recaptured white girls driven mad by their ordeal might not have been true to the norm, it emphasizes the prevailing belief that girls and women were always defiled by Indian capture. It's reminiscent of the scene in *Stagecoach* in which the gambler Hatfield holds a pistol to Lucy Mallory's head, ready to kill her if they are defeated by attacking Apaches, to save her from the proverbial fate worse than death. And that moment is identical to a scene in *The Big Trail*, evidence both of the pervasiveness of this line of thinking and of Ford's penchant for creative borrowing.

But in Cynthia Ann Parker's case, her marriage to Peta Nocona was a good one, testified to by the fact that he did not take any other wives after her, contrary to expectations for a tribal chieftain. One of their sons, Quanah, became the last great Comanche chief. Peta Nocona was killed in a raid in 1864 on the Pease River, in a virtual slaughter: most of the Comanche warriors were away at the time, so the Texas Rangers wantonly killed women and children, only sparing Cynthia when they saw that she had blue eyes. That raid is suggested in *The Searchers* by the slaughter of a small

Comanche encampment by the U.S. Cavalry, including the murder of the Native American maiden named Look who is comically
traded to Martin as a wife; she is the object of much misogynistic
humor as Martin physically throws her out of his bedroll and sends
her home. That this character is played for laughs and then slaughtered is unsettling, but it was Ford's attempt to show that there
was savagery on both sides.

The Peta Nocona of Le May's novel is twisted into Scar,
the hardened, vengeful Comanche warrior. Scar is also out for
vengeance—his sons have been slaughtered by white men—
making him Ethan's double. At the dramatic climax of the film,
Ethan and Martin take part in a cavalry raid on a village where
Scar is known to be hiding. Martin sneaks in, finds Debbie, and
rescues her. When Scar suddenly enters the teepee, Martin shoots
him, escaping with Debbie just as Ethan arrives on the scene. In a
final act of brutal vengeance, Ethan removes his knife and bends
down to scalp his dead rival—and his counterpart—becoming the
savage he has vilified throughout the film.

He then goes after Debbie. In a terrifying finale, he mounts his
rearing steed and chases her down, an armed man on horseback
pursuing a defenseless young woman on foot. At the last minute,
when he captures her, we see in her close-up that she is not like
the crazed and craven young captives at the fort. In a sudden and
dramatic reversal, Ethan takes her in his arms and says, "Let's go
home, Debbie." It's a shocking ending. His abrupt turn to tenderness and sanity completely redeems his character. As Scorsese
noted, "Ethan Edwards is not a villain. He is despicable and yet
you love him when he says, 'Let's go home, Debbie.'" Strangely,
the picture provides not the slightest hint of his monumental
about-face before this moment.

In the screenplay, Ford originally had Ethan prepare to shoot
Debbie, telling her, "I'm sorry, girl. . . . Shut your eyes," before
looking into her face and saying, "You sure favor your mother."
That moment of recognition would certainly explain his change
of heart. But Ford removed that sequence from the script, so the

✳

The surprising conclusion of *The Searchers:*
Natalie Wood as Debbie, the kidnapped girl, Wayne as
her pursuer, and Jeffrey Hunter as her adopted
brother and rescuer.

film provides no clear explanation for Ethan's actions. Did scalping Scar satisfy his bloodlust? Or did his family loyalty—and love for Martha—finally trump his blinding anger and racism? Or perhaps he could see, as the viewer does, that she is not a demented, ruined girl like the ones recently rescued by the cavalry. It's an unforgettable finale partly because it's unexpected and ambiguous, and it succeeds beautifully in part because of John Wayne, the man of rough justice who will ultimately find a way to do the right thing. His aura and his status lend credibility to this final catharsis. His sudden mercy also transforms Ethan into a father figure, albeit a harsh one. This sudden, silent forgiveness is a paternal prerogative, an act of love.

In the rescue scene, while Ethan redeems himself by sparing Debbie, Martin assumes the mantle of the heroic archetype. He is the one who kills the formidable warrior Scar and rescues his sister. Martin's growth from youthful Indian sympathizer to victor over a Comanche chief marks his becoming a man. In a brief few moments of screen time, Martin and Ethan change places: Martin finds the necessary hardness to rescue his sister, and Ethan has found the love in his heart to reject killing her.

※

Only John Wayne—and all his preexisting associations with justice and bravery—could command sympathy and respect while portraying Ethan Edwards. Repellent as his racism, and his intention to kill his niece, might be, Bogdanovich notes that "the audience doesn't hate him." In fact, to viewers he's still the hero of the picture: "The reason they like him is because he's John Wayne! You can't make John Wayne unlikable. That's what Hawks discovered."

John Ford knew that casting Wayne would add to the moral ambiguity of the story. Again, as in so many Ford Westerns, heroes are outsized. Ethan Edwards commands our attention by towering over everyone else, except for the burly Reverend Clayton. Ward

Bond and John Wayne—the two former USC football players—are well matched in size and presence. If anything, Bond is even more commanding, bigger and louder than Wayne in his role as reverend and Ranger. Like Ethan, Clayton has an easy authority, but as a reverend he also wields explicit moral influence. In an early scene in which the rescue party escapes an attack by the Comanches, he cautions Ethan to allow the Indian warriors to retrieve their dead and wounded before firing on them. He also objects when Ethan shoots out the eyes of a dead Indian warrior, condemning his spirit to wander the afterlife forever, according to Comanche tradition. It's a chilling moment, showing the blackness of Ethan's rage, and it reveals his knowledge of Indian ways, as does a scene where he wantonly shoots bison to deprive the Indians of food.

Ethan exists on the edge of two civilizations—white home-steaders and Native Americans. A whiff of the outlaw clings to him: he flashes newly minted Yankee dollars to his brother at the beginning of the movie, and Clayton suggests that Ethan fits the description of several outstanding warrants. At the end of the picture, Ethan is wanted for murder of the treacherous Futterman, a trading post owner who sells knowledge of Debbie's whereabouts to Ethan and then, after being paid, tries to rob Ethan of the gold coins he's carrying. It's interesting to note that though Ford will increasingly question the devaluation of the Native American, one of the minor but important villains in *The Searchers* is Futterman, with the suggestion that he is a Jewish merchant.

Ford took additional steps to muddy the waters, such as making Martin Pawley part Indian—not so in Le May's novel. As such he comes across, at least to mid-century American audiences, as the only fully moral character who can see both sides of the West's defining conflict. His unusual beauty and his dark skin distinguish him as a racial other, and he enters the movie riding bareback, leaping off his horse like a Plains Indian. Ethan's racism—or "trib-alism," as Curtis Hanson calls it—sets him against the youth from the start, even as Martin becomes a kind of surrogate son during their journey.

Wayne being sworn in by Ward Bond in *The Searchers*.
The two were close friends since playing
football together for USC.

Is Ford a racist, or—as Bogdanovich says about the movie—is he "picturing the complicated face of racism"? Bogdanovich points out that aside from the reverend, only the "quarter breed" Martin Pawley consistently shows compassion and humanity toward the Indians. Even Martin's girl, Laurie, angrily says that Debbie should be killed after living with the Comanches; she suggests a bullet through her head, as "Martha would want it." Out of the mouth of this young woman we see the virulent racism and fear of the other that pervades her community; Martin's perspective, and ours, and Ford's, are enlightened—and out of time.

COURTSHIP AND SLAPSTICK

The Searchers wouldn't be a John Ford film if it didn't contain both broad comedy and ritual singing and dancing. We have both when one of the homesteaders, a young swain named Charlie McCorry (Ken Curtis), decides to court Laurie in Martin's absence. With his intense blue eyes and fine features, he's as handsome as Martin, and he sings a winning "Skip to My Lou" in his beautiful baritone in his attempt to woo Martin's girl. But his thick hillbilly accent—a forerunner to Curtis's sidekick role of Festus in TV's *Gunsmoke*—makes him a comedic character, and his fancy clothes make him seem eastern and effete next to Martin, the natural man covered in dust from the trail. There should be no contest between the two suitors because Laurie has already told Martin, to his pleasant surprise, that she considers herself engaged to him since childhood. But with Martin gone for so long, and unable to express his love for Laurie, he's left the field to his loquacious rival.

Martin's long absence—seven years!—looking for Debbie has embittered Laurie. All that time she seeks some sign of his love, but the shy Martin has difficulty even writing her a letter that can convey his feelings from afar. Martin possesses all the qualities of a hero—bravery, grace under pressure, willingness to act, loyalty, the ability to take a beating and still get up—but he does not know how to court a girl, even one who has already pledged herself to him. So McCorry beats his time, wins Laurie through his attentive crooning, becomes engaged to her, and in a comic scene sets out to marry her in a festive wedding in the Jorgensen home, presided over by Reverend Clayton.

There is music and dancing, but just as we fear Martin has lost his girl, he arrives home and wins her back the only way he knows how: he fights for her. The two men roll in the mud and dust while the wedding goers urge them on, with Laurie relishing the scene of a contest over her. While their fisticuffs technically end in a draw, McCorry gives up the girl and exits the scene. And then, having won back his girl, Martin leaves again.

In many Ford Westerns, dance represents "community, tradition, ritual, and family feeling," as Bogdanovich has observed. But in *The Searchers*, the big dance at Laurie's wedding concludes in a comic fight. However, there is a more somber use of Fordian music earlier in the film, at the funeral of Aaron and Martha Edwards and their son, all killed by the Comanche war party. The homesteaders sing "Shall We Gather at the River" at graveside—Ford's favorite song, according to Bogdanovich, and the tune Borzage would routinely play on his accordion to mark Ford's appearance on the set. Here, the small community has come together to grieve, but the fragile group is quickly threatened by Ethan Edwards, who, with a posse of Texas Rangers and homesteaders, sets out to find Scar and kill him. Laurie's mother, Mrs. Jorgensen, grabs Ethan and begs him, "Don't let the boys waste their lives in vengeance." That is the unbearable crux of the film: to sacrifice home and family in order to protect home and family.

THE MAN ALONE

In the film's denouement, Ethan brings Debbie home to the Jorgensens' neighboring homestead; no indication is given that she will fail to re-assimilate like her tragic historical prototype. Martin arrives at the homestead as well, welcomed by his fiancée, Laurie. In fact, all are welcomed across the threshold, in a shot that mirrors the opening scene. But Ethan hesitates at the welcoming doorway, holding his elbow in his right hand as he turns to head back into the wilderness. It's a gesture typical of Harry Carey, to whom Ford dedicated *The Searchers* in a closing credit.

Filmmaker Curtis Hanson describes the last scene as one in which Ethan finds "peace and acceptance" by walking away. "John Wayne had the most beautiful walk in movies," he said, and that certainly adds to the poignancy of the scene, but it's a sense of necessary exclusion that lingers. The film carefully catalogs what "drives a man to wander" (in the lyrics of the opening and closing ballad), and the stark beauty of that final image transfigures the vengeful and racist Ethan Edwards, now redeemed, into a folk hero. It is an eerily beautiful image full of pathos, and it went far in defining the American hero as a loner, living on the outskirts of civilization, without family, friends, or love.

At the core of this archetype is a fear that men are most prized—and perhaps *only* prized—for their ability to protect and avenge, that they cannot function well in the wholly different kinds of dramas involved in family. For some men, being a silent protector is a refuge from the demands of domesticity and emotional relationships. But when exactly did this become a masculine ideal? Ford's early heroes worked within a community, or a family, or comrades, or a military corps, or with the help and encouragement of a girlfriend or wife; consider George O'Brien in *The Iron Horse* or Henry Fonda in *My Darling Clementine* and *Guns Along the Mohawk*. If anything, Ford's pictures celebrate male *community*, especially in his Cavalry Trilogy and even in *Stagecoach*, where the cowboy hero is part of a group of desperate travelers and a woman accompanies his bid to outrun the "blessings of civilization."

So why does Ford's greatest Western, *The Searchers*, change that dynamic? Even though Ethan Edwards is not a sympathetic character, the stunning image of him at the end of the picture, framed against the doorway of the prairie home he is leaving, the unknowable wilderness before him, is an enduring cultural touchstone. Since then, the cowboy hero—indeed, the hero writ large—

*

The iconic image of Duke Wayne's Ethan Edwards
as the outcast loner. His pose pays homage to his cowboy
hero Harry Carey, the man who launched Ford's career
as a director of Westerns.

has become the loner, the drifter, the figure set apart from society. TV Westerns embraced this model, and lone, often avenging, cowboys played by Clint Eastwood in *High Plains Drifter, Hang 'Em High*, and *The Man with No Name* marked its apotheosis. It spread into other action hero films, too, such as the *Death Wish* franchise, in which Charles Bronson becomes a lone vigilante after his wife and daughter are brutally murdered.

Ford might have been influenced by an earlier film, George Stevens's 1953 movie, *Shane*, starring Alan Ladd as the eponymous gunslinger. *Shane* romanticizes the figure of the lone Western hero who saves the day, in stark contrast to the weakened, vulnerable family man and homesteader, Joe Starrett, played by Van Heflin. Brandon de Wilde as Starrett's young son, Joey, has a classic line at the end, plaintively crying, "Shane! Come back!" as if to say, "Come back and teach us how to be men!"

But Ford's final image of Ethan's walking away is far more iconic than Shane's riding off into the sunset, in part because of its stark beauty. Shane is heroic, yes, but he is one-dimensional in ways that Ethan Edwards is not. Ethan gives a glimpse of his ability to love a woman and perhaps a child, so what he forsakes by returning to the wilderness is clear. While Martin takes Ethan's place as the new head of the family, presumably to marry his sweetheart and continue the homesteader's life, Ethan must walk away from his last chance at familial love. He's already on his way to becoming an outlaw legend, and no one comes running after him to bring him back into the golden firelit circle.

The film's conclusion is purely Ford's invention: he abandoned the shooting script's original reconciliation scene. Ethan is "the eternal outsider in that picture," observes Bogdanovich. "He'll never be part of the family. He wasn't at the beginning of the movie; he wasn't with the woman he loved." For Ford, who adored his mother and cherished the memory of growing up in a lively home of roughhousing brothers, it is a bitter ending, a darkening of his vision of the West and of the Western hero.

Part Two

A LUST
FOR
DIGNITY

5

Love and Politics

I was dancing barefoot by firelight, wearing a low-cut gypsy costume.
—PILAR WAYNE

Like many fine artists . . . [Ford's] true feeling was for
the man-man or man-men relationship.
—DUDLEY NICHOLS

The Searchers was the apotheosis of John Ford and John Wayne's artistic collaboration, the most mature expression of the Western hero they had been pursuing together for over a decade. But by 1957 the lives of the two men had been drawing apart for some time, a split that would be most clearly felt in 1960 with *The Alamo*. The roots of this rupture stretched back to Ford's happiest days during World War II—a period that was anything but happy for John Wayne.

Duke was thirty-four in 1941 when the Japanese attacked Pearl Harbor and the United States entered the war. He was beyond the age of being drafted, and he had a family to support—he was still married, unhappily, to Josephine Saenz—yet the same could be said for his fellow actors Henry Fonda, James Stewart, Clark Gable, Robert Montgomery, and Ronald Reagan, not to mention Ford, who was even older and in poor health. All of these Hollywood icons served, Ford and Jimmy Stewart with particular distinction.

Duke badly wanted to enlist, but there were complications. First, he'd just signed a new contract with Republic Pictures that gave him a lucrative percentage of the profits from any film he made, and after being in the business for nearly fifteen years, for the first time Duke stood to make considerable money. According to Duke's third wife, Pilar, when he told Republic's studio chief, Herbert Yates, that he planned to enlist, Yates responded by threatening to sue him over breach of contract. "If you don't live up to it, I'll sue you for every penny you've got," he reportedly said. "Hell, I'll sue you for every penny you hope to make in the future. God damn it! Nobody walks out on me!"

In January 1944, Duke spent three months touring the southwest Pacific for the USO. He loved entertaining the troops and came to feel that this was his contribution to the war effort. "I was America to them," he said. "They'd taken their sweetheart to the Saturday matinee as teenagers and held hands through a John Wayne Western. . . . It was better that I go into the war zones on tour" than as a soldier, he believed, and indeed he was probably right. Had he enlisted, he would have been just one lowly GI, but his status as a celebrity symbol of masculinity helped raise morale throughout the service, and his face on a recruitment poster brought in more men than any other campaign. The screenwriter Edmund Hartmann related a conversation he'd had with a nun, who said, "You know, our most decorated soldier is John Wayne." When Hartmann disagreed, tactfully pointing out that "Wayne was never in the army. He never fired a gun in earnest in his life. . . . [He] never shot anybody who didn't get up and go for coffee afterwards!" she didn't believe him.

※

Meanwhile, the glow of Ford's wartime experience lingered, and his first feature film after his Midway documentary, the 1945 World War II drama *They Were Expendable*, celebrated the camaraderie of PT boat commanders. The navy gave Ford permission to take a leave from active duty to make the film for MGM, based on a best seller by William L. White about the doomed heroism of a PT boat squadron executing General MacArthur's order to evacuate the Philippines in 1942. It was filmed in Key Biscayne, Florida, with John Wayne and Robert Montgomery in the leading roles and Donna Reed playing Wayne's love interest.

If Duke had looked up to Ford before the war, when Ford returned a hero, Duke's admiration grew to outright worship. By this point Ford had adopted his trademark black eye patch, which he wore under his tinted glasses and flipped up in order to read anything. But he was in many ways still the same old John Ford, chewing one end of a ratty handkerchief to battle his cravings for alcohol while insisting on a sober cast and crew.

By 1945, John Wayne had a solid film reputation, but unlike Ford, the decorated war hero, Duke had not served, and Ford would never let him forget it. During the filming of *They Were Expendable*, Ford constantly insulted and picked on Duke, pointing out that he didn't even know how to salute properly. One of the character actors on the film, Donald Curtis, recalled how Ford would "bully John Wayne and make a quivering pulp out of him. Ford had an honest affection for Duke, but Wayne was scared to death of him." It got so bad that Robert Montgomery—whom Ford respected because the actor was a navy man who had served honorably in the war—took the director aside and threatened to walk off the picture if he didn't let up on Duke. Ironically, when Ford injured his leg in a fall from a scaffold and Montgomery took over the task of directing for a week, Duke was upset. He didn't like the way Montgomery leaned on Ward Bond, who was recovering from a broken leg he'd sustained in an automobile accident, and he waited eagerly for Pappy to return.

The film opened in December 1945, three months after Japan

surrendered, and a war-weary public largely stayed away; the film was a financial disappointment, and Ford returned to a form for which he had an undisputed knack—the Western—with the first installment of the Cavalry Trilogy two years later. Still, *They Were Expendable* has aged well, and it marked John Wayne's first appearance on the big screen as a war hero. Indeed, by the end of the war, given his heroics in *They Were Expendable* and *Back to Bataan*, also released in 1945, the fictional John Wayne, screen icon, and Duke Wayne, private man, had merged.

But not to Duke himself: though he likely made the right decision in terms of serving his country in the most beneficial way that he could, not enlisting was a source of shame that haunted him. "He would become a 'super patriot' for the rest of his life trying to atone for staying at home," Pilar Wayne wrote in her affectionate memoir about her life with the Duke.

TRUE LOVE

Duke met the Peruvian actress and former flight attendant Pilar Pallete in the summer of 1952, when he was first scouting locations for *The Alamo.* She was then the estranged wife of an American adventurer and bush pilot named Richard Weldy, whom Duke had looked up when he arrived in Peru. Weldy took him to a remote location in Tingo María, where Pilar was filming a movie titled *Green Hell.* Later that night, cast and crew were invited to the Plaza Hotel for cocktails to meet their distinguished visitor. Pilar later recalled, "I was dancing barefoot by firelight, wearing a low-cut gypsy costume," and Duke was instantly attracted. She wasn't quite sure who Duke Wayne was—she mixed him up with Gary Cooper—but she was powerfully struck by his presence and easy authority. She described that night: "A great, pale jungle moon illuminated the night sky, candles glowed on the tables, and the soft murmur of a stream flowing a few feet away added to the atmosphere." Duke was captivated not only by her youthful, dark-haired beauty—she was twenty-two years younger than he—but by her aristocratic bearing. As the daughter of a Peruvian senator, Pilar was cultivated and elegant—a far cry from his second wife, the sexy, volatile, and heavy-drinking Esperanza "Chata" Baur.

Duke's marriage to Chata was, by many accounts, disastrous. Like Josephine and Pilar, Chata was Hispanic, an actress whom he'd met on a visit to Mexico in 1942, when he and his business manager, Bo Roos, had flown into Mexico City to scout a possible movie studio they were thinking of buying. Ward Bond, Ray Milland, and Fred MacMurray were all part of the expedition, and it was through Milland that Duke met the woman who would become his second wife.

Chata was a tempestuous beauty—a welcome change from the devout, disapproving Josephine—and by many accounts she liberated Duke sexually, but she was an alcoholic, which soon became a problem for the couple. Drinking was par for the course among Duke, Ford, and their cronies, but a woman who imbibed heavily was frowned upon and was not something Wayne knew how to handle. Pilar later wrote that Chata was "in fact . . . a high-class call girl who'd had a bit part in a Mexican film. Milland was one of her clients." But Pilar had also felt sorry for her, describing Chata as "an illegitimate child [who] had been abused by her mother's husband."

At first, Duke was infatuated with her, especially given his unsatisfying marriage to Josephine, from whom he was estranged. In June 1943, Duke's affair with Chata led Josephine to file for a legal separation. Duke wrote to John Ford about the demise of his marriage, "Anyway I don't give a four letter word, [so long as] I can see my kids," and he continued his affair with dark-haired, vivacious Chata. Later, when his divorce from Josephine was finalized, "Duke . . . walked away from the marriage with his clothes, his car, and an overwhelming feeling of guilt he never completely put behind him," Pilar later wrote. Josephine walked away with the couple's house in upscale Hancock Park in Los Angeles and 35 percent of Duke's annual earnings. And because she was a Catholic, she never considered herself divorced in the eyes of God, and

＊

John Wayne with Pilar Pallete, who would become his
third wife, at the Cocoanut Grove in Hollywood in 1949.

she let her children know that she would always consider herself John Wayne's only true wife—a situation that would, not surprisingly, create tension between Pilar and the children of his first marriage.

Chata and Duke married on January 17, 1946, in Long Beach, in a small ceremony, with Ward Bond as his best man. The couple moved into a small ranch house in Van Nuys, close to Republic studios, where Duke was producing and starring in *Angel and the Badman*, with twenty-three-year-old co-star Gail Russell. Chata, especially when drinking, became intensely jealous of the beautiful young actress, convinced that Duke was having an affair with her. She also resented the way his work consumed him. "My husband is one of the few persons who is always interested in his business. He talks of it constantly. . . . [H]e spends all of his time working, discussing work, or planning work," she reportedly said. When Chata brought her mother to live with them in an already volatile situation, it proved too much for Duke. The two women would drink together and sometimes fight, and Duke would spend as much time away from home as possible. Luckily, he was able to spend a month on location working on *Fort Apache* with John Ford.

Though Duke bought a five-acre estate with a twenty-two-room farmhouse in Encino for Chata and her mother to live in, the marriage devolved into drunken fights, mutual accusations of infidelity—he with Gail Russell, she with hotel scion Nicky Hilton—and all-around misery.

On September 12, 1952, a few months after Duke met Pilar, he and Chata filed separate divorce suits, each of them charging "physical and mental cruelty." He had moved out of their house in Encino and was living as a bachelor in an apartment on Longridge Avenue, dodging gossip hounds like Hearst's syndicated columnist Louella Parsons. When Pilar arrived in Los Angeles to dub an English version of *Green Hell*, she and Duke began an affair, in secret, so as not to give Chata additional grounds for the high maintenance alimony she was seeking—$50,000 a year for six years. And when Pilar became pregnant, knowing she couldn't be with Duke until his divorce was finalized, she sadly, reluctantly, had an abortion.

Duke's marriage to Chata had lasted seven years, and again he was filled with guilt at his failed marriage, blaming himself. "It was an embarrassing ordeal to live through," Duke later said of their all-too-public divorce, adding, "Maybe I'm still afraid of women. I am awed by their presence. I feel there is something beautiful about a fine woman. . . . I'm not complaining. I'm living in a good country. I'm doing work I love." Their divorce, finalized in October 1953, was as contentious as their marriage had been, with Chata claiming a $150,000 settlement plus the $50,000 annual maintenance, with Duke holding on to the Encino estate. They finally settled on a lump sum of $375,000.

The troubled Chata returned to Mexico City and allegedly drank herself to death at the age of thirty-eight, just thirteen months after the settlement. After his divorce from Josephine Saenz, Duke had remained close to his four children from that union—Michael, Antonia (Toni), Patrick, and Melinda—often bringing them to the sets of his movies and sometimes giving them production jobs and small roles in his pictures. His third marriage, by many accounts—especially Pilar's!—was his most loving and most enduring, lasting twenty-five years. She bore him three children—Aissa, who played the child of one of the soldier's wives in *The Alamo*; John Ethan, named after Wayne's character in *The Searchers*; and Marisa. In *The Alamo*, when Aissa is introduced to Davy Crockett, the character Wayne somewhat reluctantly assigned to himself, the love that shines from his eyes almost constitutes a break in character.

That Duke Wayne married three women of Latin American descent fueled much speculation throughout his life; some thought he sought out compliant, dependent women to marry, when in reality all three were formidable in their own right, willing and able to challenge him, in their different ways. And Chata and Pilar were very different from his cold, unloving mother who had so clearly preferred his younger brother. Duke himself explained, "To me, [Hispanic women] seem more warm and direct and down-to-earth."

✳

Ford, meanwhile, had a similarly turbulent domestic life, although for different reasons. One cannot deny the fundamental ambiguity of his artistic output: he admired big blustery men of unquestioned masculinity—hard drinking, quick to fight, passionate—but he saw that a civilizing influence would come from more moderate men, and often from women. In fact his last film, *7 Women*, employs a nearly all-woman cast. Ambiguity resided within Ford's heart, and he struggled to accept not only his artistic nature but—possibly—his own conflicted sexuality. There is evidence in his work and from those who knew him best to suggest repressed attraction to men, despite his long marriage to Mary and his apparent love affair with Katharine Hepburn.

No wonder Jack Ford worshipped Katharine Hepburn, for her boyish beauty, her forthrightness, her total candor, her absolute courage. He even did the unthinkable, once, in allowing her to direct herself in a love scene in 1936's *Mary of Scotland*, on a kind of dare. Unlike Mary, Hepburn relished Ford's Irishness, and she called him by his Irish name, Sean, which of course he loved. She liked his Irish tweed jackets and flannel trousers rolled up at the ankles, though he would wear them "until they were ready to rot. . . . His white tennis shoes were almost black; no one could remember seeing them fresh and new," in Hepburn's description. She understood his bohemianism, and she even took in stride the handkerchiefs he shredded, sucking and biting on them throughout a film shoot.

One of Hepburn's biographers, Barbara Leaming, writes that Ford proposed marriage to the actress as early as 1936, though he declined to sleep with her until Mary granted him a divorce. (Mary was a divorcée when he met him, thus they had not married in the Catholic Church.) Hepburn even wrote a personal letter to Mary offering her $150,000 if she would divorce Ford and let him keep custody of Barbara, the daughter to whom he was particularly close.

Mary refused.

There's plenty of testimony that his marriage was not a happy one. "His family life was terrible," Harry Carey Jr. told Bogdanovich, "yet it was marvelous in the movies." It wasn't that he didn't love Mary McBride Ford, his wife of many years; his letters home reveal a genuine tenderness:

> *Well, Ma, I sure fell in love with you more than ever when you spoke to me on the 'phone—you've plenty of guts, Ma, the right kind—your Aloha to a sailor going to sea was swell—I'm proud as hell of you. I'm going away feeling better than ever. . . . I pray to God it will soon be over so we can live our life together with our children + grandchildren + our "Araner"—Catalina would look good now—God bless + love you my darling—I'm tough to live with—heaven's knows + Hollywood didn't help—Irish + genius don't mix well but you do know you're the only woman I've ever loved—God bless m'darling*
>   *from*
>   *daddy*

John Ford wrote this letter to his wife, Mary, from "somewhere in Hoboken," on Office of Strategic Services letterhead when he was about to be deployed to the Pacific theater as head of the Field Photographic Branch. His letters to Mary, from Honolulu, Washington, and Panama, are full of affection: "The only things I miss are you and Barbara—it seems strange not to see you on the beach with sun-tan oil—or Babs running around in shorts in a terrible hurry to grab a sandwich or go to a movie—I guess I must love you all very much."

Their marriage lasted, but it was increasingly described as a rather passionless and remote relationship. They ended up with separate bedrooms and rather separate lives. Leaming notes that

Mary tended to belittle Ford throughout their long marriage, complaining that he should leave Hollywood and "find a manlier occupation" (she certainly knew how to best insult him!). She looked down on Ford's "shanty Irish" background and interpreted his artistic sensitivity as weakness—one of Ford's great fears—and she was able to use his tendency toward Catholic guilt as a way to manipulate him. Leaming writes, "Abuse poured constantly from Mary's lips. She accused her husband of being weak and unmanly. . . . She bemoaned his failure to leave Hollywood and seek a proper job." She also reports that Ford seemed to be "a little frightened of Mary" and even "rough-and-tumble fellows like John Wayne tiptoed around her." Though Mary Ford had grown up poor in New Jersey, she put on the airs of a southern aristocrat, lording it over her husband that she could trace her lineage to Sir Thomas More. She reportedly used her sense of social superiority to hold on to her husband, and "the more successful he became in Hollywood, the more necessary it was to remind him of his inferiority," writes Leaming, though she continued to turn up her nose at the motion picture business.

What seemed to hold the marriage together, besides their two children and Ford's Catholicism, which, for him, made divorce untenable, was their deep, mutual, unquenchable thirst. In the early years of their marriage, it was Mary who made bootleg gin in the bathtub—"three drops of juniper juice to a pint of water"—and who loved to entertain her high-spirited navy pals. They were both alcoholics, which created an indissoluble bond.

❋

Rumors of homosexuality cropped up around Ford as early as his friendship with Harry Carey, enough so that some of Ford's biographers have felt compelled to address it in various ways. Ronald L. Davis first speculated in his 1995 biography, *John Ford: Hollywood's Old Master:*

Fearful of intimacy, mistrustful of love, ashamed of sex, Ford was most comfortable with a celibate life. . . . In a different age Ford might have turned to homosexuality, but had he done so in the first half of this century, guilt would have overwhelmed him. Without question he preferred the company of men, and male bonding reached inordinate proportions. He may have been physically attracted to men on occasion, but there is no indication that he gratified his appetites homosexually.

Scott Eyman's impressive 1999 biography, *Print the Legend: The Life and Times of John Ford*, doesn't give much attention to the question of Ford's sexuality, except to note that Ford

was not, for instance, homophobic, although having been born in the last decade of the nineteenth century, and brought up Roman Catholic, it might have been expected. He regularly employed a wardrobe man who was well known as a homosexual. Ford knew it and wouldn't allow any of his stock company, some of whom were, shall we say, less than sensitive in these matters, to taunt the man.

Eyman also described Ford's close friendship with Brian Desmond Hurst, the Belfast-born set designer and later a celebrated director, who was gay and whom Ford mentored, employing him first as a chauffeur and then as an assistant director.

Joseph McBride's definitive work, *Searching for John Ford* (published in 2001), also raises the question, noting that Harry Carey "poked fun at Ford's 'infatuation with muscle' and fondness for displaying those actors' physiques," but Harry's son, Dobe, felt that his father was "not necessarily implying that Ford had homosexual tendencies." Rather, Harry Carey Sr. might have resented his replacement as a leading man by "younger, brawnier, and more handsome actors such as [Tom] Mix, George O'Brien, and John Wayne" when his contract with Universal was dropped in 1921.

But one of Harry and Ollie Carey's ranch hands, Joe Harris, who had been a member of the Ford stock company and often played heavies in Ford's silent films, spread stories with insinuations about Ford's sexuality. McBride writes, "This may have been the first time, but it would not be the last, that such gossip was inspired by Ford's sensitivity, his diffidence around women, and his admiration for good-looking he-men."

Ollie Cary dismissed such talk as mere troublemaking, but she herself once described Jack Ford as having a very effeminate walk—like most directors, she was quick to add. McBride also notes that "the gossip about Jack's masculinity was spread only after he finally, and somewhat precipitously, took the plunge into marriage."

The most specific account comes from Maureen O'Hara, who, in her 2004 memoir, *'Tis Herself*, describes walking in on Ford in the arms of an unnamed actor, most likely Tyrone Power. All three were on location in 1954 filming *The Long Gray Line* for Columbia Pictures, a movie celebrating the historical Marty Maher, an Irishman who started as a custodian at West Point, became a trainer of cadets, and ended up as commander of the military academy, starring Tyrone Power as Maher and O'Hara as his wife, Mary O'Donnell Maher. Incidentally, Duke Wayne was Ford's first choice for Maher, but his work on another film prevented his taking the role. O'Hara writes,

> I walked into his office without knocking and could hardly believe my eyes. Ford had his arms around another man and was kissing him. I was shocked and speechless. I quickly dropped the sketches on the floor, then knelt down to pick them up. I fumbled around slowly and kept my head down. I took my time so they could part and compose themselves. They were on opposite sides of the room in a flash. The gentleman Ford was with was one of the most famous leading men in the picture business. He addressed a few pleasantries to me, which were forced and awkward, then quickly

left. . . . Not a word was said, and I played it out as if I hadn't seen a thing.

"Later," she writes, "that actor approached me and asked, 'Why didn't you tell me John Ford was a homosexual?' I answered, 'How could I tell you something I knew nothing about?'"

O'Hara later speculates that Ford struggled with homosexual feelings, and it gave her insight into the problems in his marriage: "the separate bedrooms, his insulting her, the periodic drinking, and the lack of outward affection they showed to each other. I now believe there was a conflict within Ford and that it caused him great pain and turmoil."

It must be noted that O'Hara and Ford had always had a contentious relationship, though she was indeed one of his favorite actresses, co-starring in five of his films, and he seemed infatuated with her while making *The Quiet Man* in Ireland. O'Hara fulfilled his romantic notions of the feisty, independent-minded Irish. But she spoke up too often on the sets of his movies, challenging his authority, and found herself "in the barrel" on many occasions—that is, at the center of the Old Man's wrath. And then there was that time he punched her in the jaw at one of his parties, as described earlier.

"It was the fourth picture I'd made with John Ford," she writes, "and by far the most difficult. I knew the dos and don'ts. I knew about being in the barrel." But she felt that something had changed in their relationship by the time they filmed *The Long Gray Line:* "There was anger toward me and it was revealing itself in all its ugliness." He seemed determined to humiliate her in front of the cast and crew, and he greeted her each morning on the set by loudly asking, "Well, did Herself have a good shit this morning?" Between takes, he'd yell at her, "Come on! Move that big ass of yours!" She wondered if he was punishing her for, among other possibilities, her close friendship with Duke Wayne. In fact, when Wayne visited the set, Ford forbade her to speak a single word to him.

O'Hara speculated, "His fantasies and crushes on women like

me, Kate Hepburn, Anna Lee, and Murph Doyle—all of whom he
professed love for at one time or another—were just balm for his
wound. He hoped each of us could save him from these conflicted
feelings, but was later forced to accept that none of us could. I
believe this ultimately led to my punishment and his downward
spiral into an increased reliance on alcohol."

She believed that whereas Ford was accepting of homosexuality in others, he couldn't admit it in himself, for a number of
reasons—his image as a military hero and a man's man, but also his
Catholicism, which taught him that to act on those feelings was a
grievous sin. She recalls a letter Ford once sent to her when she was
in Australia, inexplicably including the following prayer:

> *Father—I love my man dearly*
> *I love him above my own life*
> *But, Father—my soul hurts me—*
> *I've never been in the same bed with him—*
> *And I want him heaven knows—*
> *Father, dear—what shall I do—*
> *Oh what shall I do?*

Was Ford—consciously or unconsciously—reaching out to O'Hara,
hoping to unburden himself or perhaps receive guidance from a
fellow Irish Catholic?

In an interview with the author, Bogdanovich dismissed Maureen O'Hara's story about finding Ford in the arms of a prominent
actor. Bogdanovich believes that O'Hara was envious of Ford's
affection for Kate Hepburn, feeling that Hepburn had supplanted
her in the director's heart. The rumored love affair between Hepburn and Ford, he feels, belies the suggestion of Ford's homosexuality or bisexuality. He remembers being present earlier, when
Jack and Mary Ford were "still in Bel Air before he moved to the
desert. When he wasn't shooting, he was usually in bed—he liked
to hang out in bed and watch TV." Bogdanovich described the butler coming in to say, "Miss Hepburn's on the phone."

"I've never seen him look so young," Bogdanovich recalls. "He suddenly said, 'Kate?' and he went into the other room to talk to her. I've never seen him so joyous."

Despite her anger at being humiliated by Ford, Maureen O'Hara also loved him in her way: she was moved by him, and she valued his direction over the years, believing he had called forth some of her greatest performances. When interviewed on camera after Ford's death in *Directed by John Ford*, she reads a eulogy to her old tormentor and fights back tears.

Betsy Palmer, then a gamine, twenty-seven-year-old stage and television actress, also appeared in *The Long Gray Line* as Kitty Carter, a modern woman who marries a West Point cadet. Ford liked her, and he cast her as a navy nurse in *Mister Roberts* that same year. Palmer, who passed away in 2015, felt that Ford treated her "like a fella . . . as if I were one of the gang." She recalled,

> He likes women sort of on the boyish side. When I did *Mister Roberts*, I remember him directing me to get more boyish all the time, and at one point I said, "Mr. Ford, I'm gonna come across as a lesbian." . . . [H]e'd bring in that little masculine side that makes it tomboyish. There are some of us women who are that way—we can climb ladders and do it comfortably. Hepburn is one, and Maureen is, in a wonderful Irish way.

But of course there are many different kinds of love. Perhaps Ford's tragedy is that he lived in a time when to have come out as a gay man would have ruined his career, particularly as a man who explored and celebrated masculine heroism. But more important, he himself rejected that image of who he, arguably, feared to be. He wanted to be seen as a man's man, and he gruffly sought to camouflage his artistic, sensitive side. It's plausible that Ford's personal struggle informed the bullying and cruelty in his public life—"an unquenchable need to dominate might be construed as a subconscious desire to ravish," writes Davis—and the self-loathing and alcoholism in his private life.

But if true, it deepened his work.

Ford's fellow Irishman the poet William Butler Yeats wrote, "We make out of the quarrel with others, rhetoric, but of the quarrel with ourselves, poetry." It may be that Ford's struggle to suppress his desires contributed to the beauty and artistry of his films. If John Wayne tended to make propaganda when he was at the helm of a picture, John Ford almost always made art.

FORD VERSUS McCARTHY

John Ford's political orientation has also long been a puzzle. Like Duke, he's easily perceived as a right-wing ultra-patriot, especially given his love of American history, his belief in Manifest Destiny, and his many war films. But such a view fails to explain his attraction to material like *The Grapes of Wrath*—a film denounced as socialist by some of his peers—in which government plays a crucial role in offsetting the brutalities of the marketplace. Then there's the pro-labor message of *How Green Was My Valley*, in which the owners of the coal mine lack all human sympathy and the miners' only hope for survival is to unionize, though at great cost. Although he was the second director to come onto the production, it was a highly personal film for Ford. The central character of Huw, the boy who narrates the story and who was played by a young Roddy McDowall, channeled much of Ford's own childhood. Like Jack Ford, Huw is the cosseted youngest boy in a large family of hearty brothers; he spends a year convalescing from childhood tuberculosis by reading the great adventure novels, falling in love with books and storytelling. And the Welsh mining family was reminiscent of Ford's own Irish immigrant roots: the physical similarity between Sara Allgood, who played the family matriarch, and Ford's own mother, Barbara Feeney, is uncanny, and Donald Crisp's performance strongly evokes Ford's father, John Feeney. When Crisp, the Welsh patriarch, sings an Irish drinking song at his daughter's ill-fated wedding, the script-writer, Philip Dunne, wanted the song to be Welsh, not Irish. "Ah, go on!" the director reportedly scoffed. "The Welsh are just another lot of micks and biddies, only Protestants!"

And consider that satiric moment in *Stagecoach*, when Gatewood, the dishonest banker absconding with funds played by a blustery Berton Churchill, puts forth a credo that is still a familiar Republican lament:

> I pay taxes to the government, and what do we get? Not even protections from the army! I don't know what the government is coming to! Instead of protecting businessmen, it pokes its nose into business. Why, they're even talking about having bank examiners, as if we bankers didn't know how to run our own banks! . . . America for Americans! The government must not interfere with business. Reduce taxes! Our national debt is something shocking. . . . What this country needs is a businessman for president!

That those fulminating words issue from the mouth of a pompous thief tells you where Ford's affinities most likely lay—at least in 1939. To Ford, a yearning for the freedom of wide-open spaces—whether Mexico or Monument Valley or aboard the *Araner*—did not mean a narrowly defined conservatism in which government was the enemy of freedom. If one can be a libertarian and a Democrat, it seems that John Ford, in roughly the first half of his career, was just that. Though Ford lurched rightward after World War II and opposed Communist expansion, he didn't share the extreme anti-Communist views of Duke Wayne and Ward Bond.

Ford famously stood up to McCarthyism, along with director Joseph Mankiewicz, at a meeting of the Directors Guild of America on October 15, 1950, at the Beverly Hills Hotel. Mankiewicz was then the guild's president, but while he was out of the country, the ultraconservative mogul Cecil B. DeMille had introduced a loyalty oath that he and his cohorts wanted to require of all guild members. DeMille accused the liberal-leaning Mankiewicz of being a Communist sympathizer, and he and his cohorts campaigned to have Mankiewicz removed as guild president. The meeting on October 15 was something of a showdown. Mankiewicz railed against the proposed mandatory loyalty oath and the Hollywood blacklist, which was already destroying careers in Hollywood and had support from John Wayne, Ward Bond, and Ronald Reagan. DeMille accused Mankiewicz's supporters of subversion, implying that they were in the pocket of anti-American organizations and were "foreign-born" ("Jewish"), which automatically made them suspect in certain quarters of post–World War II America.

Ford sat on the sidelines throughout the heated discussion, until he finally rose, lit his pipe, and identified himself to the meeting's stenographer. "I'm John Ford," he said, with oft-quoted terseness. "I make Westerns." He looked at Cecil B. DeMille and delivered the following left-handed compliment:

> I don't think there is anyone in this room who knows more about what the American public wants than Cecil B. DeMille—and he certainly knows how to give it to them. In that respect I admire him.

He followed that up with this:

> But I don't like you, C.B. I don't like what you stand for, and I don't like what you've been saying here tonight. Joe [Mankiewicz] has been vilified, and I think he needs an apology. . . . I believe there is only one alternative, and I hereby so move: that Mr. DeMille and the entire board of directors resign and that we give Joe a vote of confidence. And then let's all go home and get some sleep. We've got some pictures to make tomorrow.

The motion was seconded and carried. Ford, and Mankiewicz, had won, though in Ford's case not out of devotion to liberal politics but out of resentment that the House Un-American Activities Committee (HUAC) should be poking its nose into Hollywood's affairs and ruining screenwriters' reputations and livelihoods. After being restored by Columbia Pictures in 1962, one such disgraced writer, Marguerite Roberts, would go on to write *True Grit*.

BIG JIM McLAIN

While Ford's political conservatism was threaded with genuine sympathy for the struggles of the laboring class, not so Duke's, which sprang from distrust, even hatred, of anything that smelled like Communism (his bosom buddy Ward Bond felt similarly and was even more vehemently right-wing than Wayne). Before World War II, Duke had considered himself an independent with a liberal bent, and he'd even voted for Franklin D. Roosevelt. But after the war, his politics lurched dramatically rightward. In 1952, Duke followed up his role in the sublimely satisfying *The Quiet Man* with the polemical *Big Jim McLain;* it was his first time out as a producer, a role he shared with Robert Fellows, a Ford acolyte. Wayne had served as producer for his movies for Republic Pictures, but now with his new production company he had the freedom to choose the stories he wanted to tell and how to tell them. This first effort amounted to little more than a work of propaganda in which Duke appeared alongside his doppelgänger, a young James Arness. The movie gives full-throated support to McCarthyism and warns against the rising tide of Communism.

Wayne plays an operative for the government sent to Hawaii to expose a Communist spy ring and haul the villains in front of HUAC, which is characterized in James Edward Grant's screenplay as a House committee that is "undaunted by the vicious campaign of slander launched against them," a reversal of the situation in which so many actors, writers, and intellectuals were slandered and lost lifetime employment—screenwriter Dalton Trumbo being a well-known example—just by being called up in front of the committee. The Communists in *Big Jim McLain* are mostly

✳

James Arness and John Wayne in *Big Jim McLain*, 1952.

bad guys from central casting—blue-collar thugs and oily, vaguely European- or Jewish-looking egghead types, including a hapless economics professor (emblematic of the growing mistrust of academics among conservatives). It's a slanted and simplistic view of Communist infiltration and a paean to HUAC, the witch hunt with anti-Semitic underpinnings that history would roundly discredit.

Even in 1952, when it premiered, *Big Jim McLain* was criticized for being overt propaganda. "One wonders about the future of his country when this sort of tripe passes for Americanism," as one particularly harsh, but not atypical, review put it. It was a daunting failure for both Duke and his screenwriter, James Grant, who had written a number of films in which John Wayne appeared, beginning with one of Duke's first productions, *Angel and the Badman* in 1947, and including *Sands of Iwo Jima*. Duke felt that Grant wrote the kind of direct dialogue that suited his way of speaking, and the two men would ultimately collaborate on ten films, remaining close friends for the rest of their lives. But *Big Jim McLain* was an undisputed dud. Though the picture lost money, Duke was convinced that it had helped to reelect Senator Joseph McCarthy, who had spearheaded investigations that destroyed careers in Hollywood. Duke had considered McCarthy a friend, saying, "Whether he went overboard or not, he was of value to my country."

The following year, Duke co-produced with Fellows the more entertaining *Hondo*, a Western that also found ways to express Duke's conservative views. In *Hondo*, Wayne's title character, a U.S. Cavalry dispatcher who had lived with the Apaches for five years, refuses to feed or make friends with a dog, Sam, that has attached himself to the tough loner because that would interfere with the dog's inherent freedom. Dogs (and men) run free—or ought to. *Hondo* is far superior to *Big Jim McLain* in story, look, content, and artistry. Though this was very much a John Wayne production, he ended up relying on his old mentor when the director, John Farrow, had to leave the production before the picture was completed. John Ford came in to direct the last few scenes, including an Apache attack on a circling wagon train.

This improvement over Wayne's previous film is not due solely to John Ford's small contribution. The setting and narrative context are crucial to its success. Wayne is simply more likable and believable in Westerns than in modern-dress pictures. As a middle-aged man, he looks bulky and over-the-hill in civilian clothes. Though he's as famous for his war pictures—*They Were Expendable, Back to Bataan, The Longest Day, Sands of Iwo Jima*—as he is for his Westerns, the John Wayne of public imagination has his face framed by the western landscape; a casually knotted neckerchief; a tall hat and boots; a slow, rolling walk with the hint of a swagger; a Winchester rifle held easily in one hand; a commanding presence straddling a horse. And timeless western garb best expresses Duke's iconic image, giving him the stature of an American tall-tale legend like Pecos Bill, or more to the point Paul Bunyan, given Duke's epic size and strength. It's pure Americana, unlike his more realistic portrayals in then-contemporary war films.

THE MENTOR

In *Hondo*, Duke portrays a much more likable character than Jim McLain, in a more compelling story, in part because he is able to present the villains of the piece—a party of renegade Apaches led by a fierce warrior—in a more balanced, realistic, and nuanced way. Falling in love with a prairie wife, Angie Lowe, played by the great stage actress Geraldine Page in her film debut, also goes a long way toward humanizing Hondo. Angie has been abandoned by her feckless husband, so Hondo looks out for her young son, Johnny, played by Lee Aaker. He teaches the boy to fish, tells him the proper names of the trout he catches, instructs him in gun safety, and orders him to be wary of Sam, Hondo's half-wild, self-sustaining dog. When he discovers that the boy cannot swim, Hondo throws him in a river stream and tells him to grab handfuls

✻

John Wayne with the brilliant Geraldine Page
in *Hondo*, 1953.

of water until he reaches the other side—an example of the kind of "tough love" that Wayne would come to embody.

The instruction of a boy in the ways of men is a larger theme of *Hondo;* when Vittorio, the chief of the marauding Apaches played by Michael Pate, discovers that Johnny's father has abandoned the family, he insists that Angie take an Apache husband so her son can be instructed in the ways of an Apache brave. Later, when he captures Hondo and is about to kill him, he only spares his life because he mistakes Hondo for Johnny's father.

It's this role as a teacher and protector of youth that completes the image of Duke as the quintessential American male. One can speculate that Ford saw that mentoring capacity in him, and given his own sentimental view of family life, he found ways to use it, notably in *3 Godfathers* and *She Wore a Yellow Ribbon.* The irony, of course, is that Pappy Ford was often a cruel father and a neglectful husband who almost always preferred the company of men over time spent with his family. Though his letters show genuine affection for his wife, and he did share a bond with his daughter, Barbara (who became an alcoholic like her father), he was known to be harsh and belittling toward his only son, Patrick, ultimately disowning him. Duke, on the other hand, forged especially close and supportive relationships with his children from two different marriages.

Mentors are rare in cinematic action and Western heroes. They don't appear in the films of Gary Cooper and seldom in Clint Eastwood's. Non-Western action heroes like Errol Flynn, Stewart Granger, Chuck Norris, Mel Gibson, Bruce Willis, Sylvester Stallone, and Arnold Schwarzenegger are more likely to have buddies than boys (or girls!) who need mentoring and guidance. A notable exception is the protective relationship between Léon, played by Jean Reno, and twelve-year-old Mathilda, played by a young Natalie Portman in her screen debut, in *The Professional.* When the tough man of action is also a nurturer, it's a winning combination and would be more fully explored in three of Duke's last films: *The Cowboys, True Grit,* and *The Shootist.*

6

Lost Battles

That picture lost so much money I can't buy a pack of chewing gum
in Texas without a co-signer.
—JOHN WAYNE

Well, Wayne was the central character, the motivator of the whole thing.
—JOHN FORD

REMEMBER *THE ALAMO?*

Duke Wayne's 1960 epic movie depicting the heroic fight for a
Republic of Texas wrested from Mexico was a full-voiced celebration of American patriotism—and it nearly ruined him. It also
marked a shift in his adoring relationship with John Ford. It would
establish Duke's independence from the tough old taskmaster; by
1960, he was referring to Ford no longer as Coach or Pappy but as
the Old Man.

In 1949, Duke had formed the production company Batjac
(named after a trading company in the 1948 picture *Wake of the
Red Witch*) to produce *Big Jim McLain* and *Hondo*. Duke planned
to make a film celebrating the heroic but disastrous loss of the

Alamo Mission in 1836 after a thirteen-day siege by the Mexican army. He'd begun serious work on the project in 1946, consulting with Texas folklorist J. Frank Dobie. From Ford he'd no doubt learned that America's spirit resided in its folktales and legends. He saw the "Texians" and their fellow defenders' brave fight against Mexican president General Antonio López de Santa Anna's vastly superior army—roughly fifteen hundred troops against barely a hundred rebels and a handful of late recruits—as an echo of America's rebellion against the British. Duke hoped his movie would serve as a reminder that America had often fought valiantly to preserve its freedom, but he overlooked the fact that the struggle accelerating in Vietnam was not a struggle for American independence, nor could it be framed as a moral imperative, like World Wars I and II, with world peace and stability imperiled. In the mind of superpatriot John Wayne, whenever and wherever America fought, it was a just fight for American values, regardless of circumstances.

Duke had begun scouting locations for *The Alamo* early, while he was still under contract to Republic Pictures. He hoped to use land just outside Panama City, but Republic's chief, Herb Yates, began to chafe at the anticipated high costs of production. His reluctance encouraged Duke to break with the studio and strike out on his own; not only would he produce the film, but he decided he would direct it as well.

Ford was against it.

Of course he knew what awaited Duke in his directorial debut; this was going to be not a small, personal movie but an epic film with choreographed battle scenes, two thousand extras, and fourteen hundred horses. Neither Ford nor Fellows thought Duke could pull it off. Perhaps Ford's competitive spirit made him ambivalent about his protégé succeeding in the directorial arena. He had helped shape Duke into a powerful screen presence and the most successful box office draw in the world for several consecutive years; that wasn't enough for his onetime third property boy?

Between various other acting projects, Duke continued to search for an ideal place to film *The Alamo*. He moved his sights from Panama to Mexico, but in 1956 he met a Texas rancher and contractor named James T. "Happy" Shahan. Shahan convinced Duke that he had to film his movie on location in Texas, offering up his own vast acreage just north of Brackettville, a small dusty town near the Mexican border. Shahan's twenty-thousand-acre ranch was the perfect setting, but the cost of building a set proved astronomical. Duke hired hundreds of Mexican laborers to build a replica of the Alamo Mission and old San Antonio as they appeared in the nineteenth century under Mexican rule. Construction ran to $1.5 million, jeopardizing the movie's budget before filming even began. Wells were dug and electric cables installed. Then there were the fourteen hundred horses and saddles that were needed, along with buckboards, cannons, and set interiors. Duke housed his cast and crew of 350 at nearby Fort Clark's barracks, and when that wasn't enough, he rented thirty-eight motel rooms. The pressure was enormous, and he began smoking nearly a hundred cigarettes a day. He found himself exploding in fury under the pressure, not unlike his mentor, John Ford. "He ate, slept, and dreamed that picture," Patrick Wayne recalled.

Duke began courting Texas millionaires to cover the skyrocketing costs and, beyond that, hocking his life to finance his movie. He mortgaged his automobiles and his home in Encino as well as a condominium he owned in New York. If this movie didn't recoup its expenses, John Wayne would be ruined.

Following Ford's example, Duke relied on many of his family members to take on crucial roles for *The Alamo:* besides little Aissa, Duke's brother, Bob, worked as a producer's aid; Duke's son Michael was an assistant producer; his son Patrick was given a small role in the movie; and his daughter Toni from his first marriage had a part in the film as well. His wife, Pilar, who seemed to have abandoned any ambition for a serious theatrical career after marrying Duke, accepted a role as an extra.

Duke also relied on several of Ford's family members and

associates: Ford's son, Patrick, wrote an early screenplay (which was not used), and the cinematographer William Clothier, who had worked with Ford on numerous films, came on board. Ford's son-in-law, Ken Curtis, took the rather colorless secondary role of Captain Dickinson, and roles were given to Olive Carey, Hank Worden, who had played the tetched-in-the-head Mose Harper in *The Searchers*, and Victor McLaglen's wife, Veda Ann Borg, in a small but memorable part as the blind wife of one of the Alamo's defenders.

Not only would Duke produce and direct the film, but in order to satisfy United Artists, the film's distributor, Duke had to star as well. United Artists put $12 million into what was at the time the most expensive Hollywood movie yet made, and Wayne's participation in a leading role was designed to guarantee that it would recoup its investment. Duke had originally thought about playing the smaller role of Sam Houston, the soldier, politician, and first president of the Republic of Texas, but the pressure from the studio left only three options: the Alamo's troop commander William B. Travis, the legendary Jim Bowie, or the frontiersman and three-term congressman Davy Crockett.

Richard Boone, the rugged, eloquent actor best remembered as Paladin in TV's *Have Gun, Will Travel*, was cast as Sam Houston, who is unable to bring his troops to the Alamo to assist Travis and his vastly outnumbered men. Travis, who is portrayed as something of an eastern-trained martinet along the lines of Henry Fonda's Colonel Thursday in *Fort Apache*, was played by the English actor and former Shakespearean Laurence Harvey, providing a sharp contrast to the hillbilly Tennesseans and rough frontiersmen who make up the Alamo's fighting corps. Jim Bowie—inventor of the outsized, eponymous knife—is portrayed as cantankerous and bellicose by a like-minded Richard Widmark. Although Widmark was shorter and slighter than Duke and many of the men assembled to defend the mission, Bowie's huge knife worn conspicuously on his belt precludes any questions about his manliness.

Duke would probably have been more believable as Jim Bowie

or Sam Houston, and he seems a bit old, heavy, and creaky in the part of the canny and likable Davy Crockett. But he understood the man whose folksy way of talking belied a keen intelligence, and in one scene he proves that he can drop the Tennessee talk and speak with studied eloquence when necessary—just as Duke taught himself to say "ain't" early on and copy the walk and talk of stuntmen and cowboys he'd hung around with in his salad days. Wayne is suited to the role in another way: Crockett was famous in his day, greeted everywhere by strangers with friendly admiration, which he graciously shrugged off. By 1960, Duke had been famous—and admired—for well over a decade, and he, too, could be graciously humble in the public eye. And perhaps he alone could pull off the feat of wearing that impressive raccoon pelt on his head throughout the entire picture.

But soon the production was $4 million over budget, and that's when John Ford stepped in.

✳

By the end of the 1950s, Ford's brilliant career was winding down, and his health and his eyesight had noticeably deteriorated. He was still cantankerous, still the alpha male in any group, but he was tired, aware that the motion picture industry was rolling on without him as the old studio system crumbled. In the new, more permissive climate dawning with the 1960s, movies often served up more sex and violence than he could stomach. One of his usual stuntmen, Chuck Roberson—known as "Bad Chuck" to distinguish him from the stuntman Chuck Hayward, known as "Good Chuck"—recalled that Ford "had always been growly with us, but now there was an edge of bitterness to him that seemed to dominate his personality."

Ford's own work broke new ground, too, but critics and audiences were not impressed. In 1959 he directed his 118th picture, *Sergeant Rutledge*, in Monument Valley. The film was ahead of its time: the hero, Sergeant Rutledge, played by Woody Strode, is a black cavalry officer wrongly accused of raping a white woman; he flees rather than face what he knows will be a biased military trial. "It was the first time we had ever shown the Negro as a hero," Ford said about the picture. But it would receive a frosty reception in the spring of 1960. Some critics felt it had not gone deep enough into racial issues, and the film lacked some of Ford's usual panache because much of it took place in a courtroom without the vast landscapes and physical derring-do that his films had become known for. After completing filming *Sergeant Rutledge* in September 1959, Ford was suddenly at loose ends. Following his usual practice, once the picture was completed, he took to his bed and drank himself into a stupor. He'd wear his pajamas all day and let his hair and fingernails—now yellowed by nicotine—grow long.

It took Duke Wayne's picture to jolt him out of his lethargy. He heard about Duke's grand ambitions in Brackettville and decided that his protégé would need his help, regardless of the fact that it was unasked for. "I hope to go to Texas to cast a paternal eye on Duke Wayne," he wrote to a friend. "This young and ambitious lad of fifty-six years [*sic*] is writing, producing, acting, and directing *The Alamo*." So he showed up in Brackettville in December, uninvited, and plopped down in the director's chair, interrupting a scene Duke was directing. "Jesus Christ, Duke, that's not the way to do it," was his only comment.

Ford hung around for days, barking orders and pretty much trying to take over the production, while Duke, naturally, resented the challenge to his directorial authority. He asked his cinematographer, William Clothier, how he should handle the situation. If it had been anybody else, Duke would have handed him his head, but he was still respectful of his most important mentor and friend of over thirty years. Clothier came up with a brilliant solution: Why not send Ford out to do the second camera sequences, keeping him out of Duke's way?

Ford obliged, working with two hundred Mexican extras who stood in as Santa Anna's soldiers; they were bused in across the border each day and then sent home at night, because they were virtually working as illegal immigrants. A single scene of the soldiers marching with bayonets along a river ended up being the only footage shot by Ford that made it into the final cut. Ford was wounded by that fact, but it was something Duke felt he had to do; he didn't want the Old Man taking over his picture, but he knew he owed him a great debt. Clothier recalled, "I don't think we used three cuts that the Old Man did." That second unit subterfuge cost Duke's production company an additional $250,000, but it was an act of diplomacy that soothed Duke's conscience, and if Ford ever suspected that he was just being placated, he didn't let on.

Seeing the tremendous strain Duke was under, Pilar was frightened for her husband. "He had put every penny he had on the line for this film and wanted to do it so badly. But I saw him going through such anguish." Duke had put his soul and heart into the picture that came closest to expressing his patriotism and his deeply held political beliefs, risking his lifelong friendship with his mentor and witnessing the Old Man's decline. Success was anything but certain.

Duke set out to dramatize a concept articulated by his character in the movie as "the eternal choice of all men—to endure oppression or resist"—and to celebrate the valor of the doomed combatants and their wives. The men are by turns blustery, comic, ornery, and loyal, but what unites them is their willingness to die for what they believe in. William Travis has that resolve from the beginning; Bowie—in bitter rivalry with his co-commander, Travis—plans to abandon the Alamo when he realizes what a lost cause it is. He persuades Crockett to gather his ragtag band of Tennessee fighters and leave with him, until—at the turning point of the film—Travis challenges them to stay. In one of the most dramatic moments of the picture, Travis marks a line in the earth and asks those who would join him to cross it. Bowie—surprisingly—buries his anger at Travis and crosses over. Several Tennesseans follow, one by one, with Crockett then dismounting from his horse and crossing over—not immediately, but perhaps realizing that if his men are willing to die in what they see as a just cause, then he

Richard Widmark, Duke Wayne, and Laurence Harvey
in Wayne's 1960 directorial debut, *The Alamo*, the epic that
nearly bankrupted Wayne.

must as well. That noteworthy moment of hesitation shows the uncertainty in a man we're supposed to admire for unfailing courage. It's a moment that makes Duke's character more human and less of a stereotypical folk hero.

An earlier scene with Jim Bowie serves a similar humanizing function. Bowie, angered by his struggle for supremacy with Travis, is suddenly informed that his wife has died of cholera in the distant town to which he'd dispatched her for safety's sake. Guilty and heartbroken, he weeps at news of her death. He blames himself for being unable to protect her and for sending her away to meet her doom. Throughout the film, Bowie is portrayed as the most stereotypically macho of the three men, renowned for his fighting, his temper, and even his drinking—when we first see him, he's hungover from a drunken night—yet in this scene we see him weeping in grief. Crockett responds with silent sympathy for his friend's bitter loss, but then he says, "Hold your head up, Jim." It's acceptable to weep, but one must recover, at least publicly.

✳

Despite Ford's admiration for the final cut—"It will last forever, run forever, for all peoples, all families everywhere"—the picture was a flop. First, the movie was just too long: 192 minutes with an intermission. Reviewers and much of the public reacted negatively to the movie's jingoistic message, with screenwriter James Edward Grant, who had also written *Big Jim McLain* and *Hondo*, taken to task for an overly sentimental, pretentious, and long-winded screenplay. An aggressive publicity campaign headed by Russell Birdwell, who'd successfully promoted David O. Selznick's *Gone with the Wind* and Howard Hughes's *Outlaw*, met resistance, in part because there was some resentment that John Wayne had simply, hubristically, taken on too much. At 20th Century Fox, Darryl Zanuck groused, "I have great affection for Duke Wayne, but what right has he to write, direct, and produce a motion picture?"

The movie ended up being nominated for seven Academy

Awards, including Best Picture and Best Supporting Actor for Chill Wills, in a small but colorful role as a Kentucky backwoods fighter, but Wills's over-the-top campaign to win his Oscar rubbed the Academy of Motion Picture Arts and Sciences the wrong way; *The Alamo* won in only one category, Best Sound.

Duke was devastated. He had hoped that *The Alamo* would "reawaken American patriotism," relying on the unquestioned heroism of men like Davy Crockett, William Travis, and Jim Bowie and using his own considerable clout and star power to make the case. He also saw it as a rebuke to the country's increasing reluctance to engage the Vietcong, and by proxy the Chinese Communists, in Vietnam. Pilar Wayne saw that *The Alamo* was his "response to all the flag burners, draft dodgers, and the fainthearted who didn't believe in good, old-fashioned American virtues." Instead, Duke had not only nearly bankrupted himself, having to sell his share of the picture back to United Artists to clear the millions he owed, but put everything he knew about filmmaking, and everything he cared about in his personal life, on the screen. He was physically exhausted, and he'd lost money in other arenas: the $375,000 divorce settlement to Chata, and a $600,000 investment in a shrimping operation in Panama that eventually failed. Before *The Alamo*, Duke estimated his worth to be around $4 to $5 million; after 1961, he was virtually ruined. To add to his burdens, Ward Bond—his closest friend and cohort in nineteen movies, who had grown up in the business with him—died suddenly at the age of fifty-seven of a massive heart attack. Dark days loomed.

Despite the poor critical and popular reception of *The Alamo*, Duke Wayne would drive even further to the right, to the point of joining the John Birch Society. His obsession with politics, combined with his workaholic approach to filmmaking, weighed on his third and happiest marriage, threatening to derail it. Pilar came to believe that his ultra-patriotism and extreme conservatism were compensation for his guilt over not fighting in World War II.

It didn't help Duke's mood that the film that won the Best Picture Academy Award in 1961, easily beating out *The Alamo*, was about as foreign to Duke's sensibilities as could be: Billy Wilder's comedic drama *The Apartment*. Starring Jack Lemmon as a junior corporate cog-in-the-wheel who tries to please his bosses by lending his apartment to them for extramarital trysts, it ushered in a new kind of man: the ill-at-ease, alienated company man or "Marketplace Man"—cut off from family, nature, valor, and often love. Shirley MacLaine co-stars as the waifish elevator operator Jack Lemmon falls for, only to discover that she's having an affair with his boss. It's classic, sublime Billy Wilder, far more reflective of its time than anything John Wayne was appearing in.

Darker still, Duke Wayne had lost thirty pounds over the ordeal of making *The Alamo*, and—now a five-pack-a-day smoker—he had started coughing up phlegm. After Ward Bond's early death, Duke's daughter Aissa later observed that "death was more than a dismal abstract for my father. It had stolen his friends and darkened his world." Nonetheless, he threw himself even harder into his work, taking just about any picture that came his way. He had losses—big losses—to recoup.

"THE HERO DOESN'T WIN, THE WINNER ISN'T HEROIC"

John Ford's 1962 film, *The Man Who Shot Liberty Valance*, is his farewell to the genre that he most identified with and through which he was able to express his great, bittersweet vision of American immigrants moving west, bringing to the frontier the blessings of civilization. It's not only Ford's last Western; it's arguably his last great picture. Ford would go on to direct five more feature films, but by the post-studio era of the early 1960s it had become difficult for him to find funding—and wide audiences—for his movies. As with *The Quiet Man*, he needed the help of his former protégé to guarantee that *Liberty Valance* would make money.

As for Duke, after losing his shirt on *The Alamo* and seeing the fruits of his long career all but disappear under his business manager Bo Roos's negligence, the veteran actor was nearly broke. "I'd worked twenty years for no gain," he realized, to his considerable dismay. But he *hadn't* worked for nothing; his reputation and his popularity continued to hold firm. Paramount came to the rescue, offering Duke a contract for ten pictures at a guaranteed salary of $600,000. *Liberty Valance* would be the first picture under his new contract with the studio, after he fulfilled a commitment to star in *The Comancheros* for 20th Century Fox, for $2 million— thus easing some of his losses.

But Duke continued to be haunted by the specter of financial ruin, something he'd witnessed firsthand growing up when his father failed in the pharmaceutical business and ended up moving the family to a hardscrabble farm in the California desert—a place Duke had hated.

"I was scared to death that I would never have financial security again, and I put that before all else, even though I thought I was doing it for the good of all my family," Duke said, not recognizing at the time that his relationship with Pilar, now pregnant again after three miscarriages, was strained to the breaking point. Not surprisingly, Pilar's miscarriages had left her depressed, and with Duke working around the clock to restore their finances, she felt alone and abandoned. She turned to charity work, becoming involved with SHARE, which raised funds for disabled children, but the more Duke became obsessed with work and with restoring his financial well-being, the more isolated she felt. Pilar didn't doubt that he loved and respected her. Duke once said, "I'll tell you why I love her. I have a lust for her dignity." But he continued to work relentlessly to support Pilar and his beloved daughter Aissa, as well as providing financial support for his first wife and their four children. Aissa later recalled her father's long absences, which he tried to make up for by showering expensive presents on his wife and daughter. In her memoir of growing up as the daughter of a legend, Aissa recalled her father saying, " 'If I don't make this movie, we're all gonna be hurting.' I never quite knew if he was telling the truth when he pleaded poverty, or if we were really in trouble."

Ford was hired by Paramount to direct *The Man Who Shot Liberty Valance*, with John Wayne starring alongside James Stewart. Lee Marvin, who had first worked with Duke as a gunrunner in *The Comancheros*, was cast as the sadistic bully and outlaw Liberty Valance.

The film pits the "new man," a country lawyer turned U.S. senator, against the heroic gunman, while eulogizing the end of the western frontier. It's a film of tribute and of loss; befitting its elegiac tone, it's shot in black and white, which Ford preferred because it "looked more like photography" and was able to convey a more somber mood than Technicolor. Unlike many of Ford's earlier masterpieces, this film was shot not out on location but at Paramount's Hollywood studio. William Clothier, a veteran of many of Ford's and Duke's pictures, offered a simple explanation: "There was one reason and one reason only why the film was shot in black and white and on Paramount's soundstages," instead of Ford's usual, majestic landscapes. "Paramount was cutting costs. Otherwise we would have been in Monument Valley or Bracketville [*sic*] and we would have had color stock. Ford had to accept those terms or not make the film." The lack of grand, Fordian vistas left the picture with a closed-in, somewhat cramped feel, but that lack of dimension actually adds to one of the film's major themes: the end of the vast American frontier.

The constricted budget might also have added to increased tensions on the set, where Ford and Wayne clashed incessantly. Filming *Liberty Valance* was not a happy experience. Perhaps because Ford knew he needed Duke to guarantee the profitability of the movie, he continued to resentfully ride him on the set. Lee Van Cleef, who plays one of Liberty Valance's henchmen, recalled how

> Ford was a complete bastard to Wayne. He'd abuse him and swear at him and call him a "goddamn lousy actor" . . . intent on humiliating the guy who got him the job of mak-

Ford directing Duke on the set of *Liberty Valance*.

ing that film, because Paramount said that if he couldn't get Wayne . . . they wouldn't back the film. And that's probably why he treated Duke that way. He didn't want to think he was doing *him* any favors.

This likely didn't rile Duke, who was no longer an inexperienced actor, as he had been on *Stagecoach* and countless earlier films, nor did Ford need to shame Duke into turning out a good performance; as a well-seasoned and a highly successful actor, he knew exactly what he was doing. But Ford did cruelly needle the one wound that still stung: he insulted and humiliated Duke for not having fought in World War II, unfavorably comparing him with Jimmy Stewart, who had had a distinguished war record.

Woody Strode recalled Ford asking Jimmy Stewart in front of Duke, "How many times did you risk your life over Germany, Jimmy?" and then asking Duke, "How rich did you get while Jimmy was risking his life?" Clothier was aware that Ford wasn't happy about accepting Paramount's strict terms of production, and he "was in a foul mood, creating tension on the set between actors, treating Duke worse than he ever did, just being a real son of a bitch."

As usual, Duke just took the abuse, although in Strode's words Ford "rode Wayne so hard, I thought he was going to go over the edge." Bogdanovich later commented that some of the abuse could be explained as Ford's way of keeping control of the production, especially because Duke now had far more clout in the movie business than did Ford. "He beat up on Duke because Duke could take it," he said, but it's interesting to note that he did not pick on Lee Marvin, a former marine and as tough a man as the many characters he played on-screen.

A NEW KIND OF HERO

Liberty Valance begins with a train pulling in to the station, its billows of steam signaling power and grandeur. On board is Senator Ransom "Ranse" Stoddard played by Stewart, who arrives at the former frontier town of Shinbone to attend the funeral of his old friend Tom Doniphon, a tough rancher and gunman played by Duke. Shinbone is a far cry from the dusty backwater it used to be, bustling now with Model Ts and other newfangledness. The steam engine is a reminder that the laying of the great transcontinental railroad was the beginning of the end of the Wild West, bringing with it the end of the outlaw era. It also calls to mind Ford's great early silent film *The Iron Horse:* the triumphal expansion of the railroad celebrated in that earlier film assumes a darker cast in *Liberty Valance*, ironic and wistful. This is one of the first Westerns to challenge the legend of the West, which, no matter how gloriously adhered to in print and in film, was often far from the cold truth of fact. Life on the frontier was often nasty, brutish, and short, a view not regularly explored until revisionist Westerns started to appear in the late 1960s. This trend toward historical realism continues today, finding its apotheosis in the cable television series *Deadwood*.

Ford also pays tribute to *Stagecoach*, his first great Western of the sound era, when Stoddard, the lawyer turned senator, stops to admire the old stagecoach, now a museum relic, which had first brought him to the frontier town twenty-five years earlier. This brief moment of contemplation is significant; it triggers the flashback that tells the entire story. And *Liberty Valance* employs three of the same players who were in *Stagecoach*—Duke, John Carradine as Major Starbuckle, a rival candidate for the state delegation, and Andy Devine as the comic and cowardly town marshal Link Appleyard. With these nods to his first important Western, Ford consciously completes the full circle of his historical and mythological American frontier saga.

In Stoddard's flashback, he is freshly arrived out west to hang up his shingle as a young attorney, in an attempt to bring law and order to the unruly frontier town. He will also bring literacy to many of the townspeople, including Hallie, the love interest of both Stoddard and Doniphon, played by Vera Miles. He doesn't carry a gun, and though Stoddard ultimately prevails, Ford feminizes him: after being stripped of all his worldly goods by Liberty Valance in a daring stagecoach robbery, Stoddard dons an apron for much of the picture as a lowly dishwasher in a local café.

The sight of an aproned Jimmy Stewart, sweeping up and washing dishes to pay his board, amplifies the contrast between the lawyer and the older rancher and gunfighter played by Duke Wayne. Stoddard is of course the object of ridicule by Liberty and his nasty sidekicks, the menacing character actor Lee Van Cleef and the comically loquacious, southern-fried Strother Martin. But it doesn't take long to discover that this feminized easterner who arrives not knowing how to shoot a gun is nonetheless feisty and full of courage. He stands up to Liberty Valance even while he's being robbed and beaten by him. Ford reportedly whispered in the actor's ear, "Jimmy, you are not a coward," to give him the motivation for that scene. Stoddard's weapons are moral indignation and an abiding belief in the law, but he'll find that they don't count for much in the frontier town of Shinbone when faced with armed psychopaths like Liberty Valance and his two depraved cohorts. However, courage *does* count, even without handiness with a gun.

The contrast between Stoddard and Doniphon extends beyond their backgrounds and mentalities, eventually presenting every other character with a choice. In a touching subplot, Doniphon is building an extra room to his frontier ranch house so he can marry Hallie, his intended—another one of Ford's tough-minded, outspoken women—and bring her home. But Stoddard has opened up new worlds to Hallie by teaching her to read and by showing her that there are other ways of securing justice besides brutal force. While keeping a soft spot in her heart for Doniphon, she will marry this new kind of hero.

Just as Hallie has to choose between her two suitors, so must Shinbone decide between remaining an unfenced territory to satisfy the cattle barons, or voting for statehood to satisfy the townspeople. The requirements of civilization press hard, and the

＊

Duke Wayne as the gunslinger and James Stewart as
the frontier lawyer, signaling the end of the Wild West,
in *The Man Who Shot Liberty Valance*, 1962.

people ultimately vote for statehood, meaning they must select their delegate to Washington.

But Stoddard, the new man, cannot simply stick around and wait to be chosen as the path forward for Shinbone. He must prove himself. As the sneering bully—played with churlish glee—continues to torment the aproned lawyer, it becomes clear that they will have to fight it out. Here Doniphon steps in and teaches Stoddard how to handle a gun, even though by now he's realized that he's losing Hallie to the young lawyer. It's another mentoring role for John Wayne, teaching the inexperienced lawyer to aim true, but a more complex one due to their mutual interest in Hallie. When Doniphon plays a trick on Stoddard by having him shoot a can of paint that completely splatters him, Stoddard punches Doniphon in the jaw. Again, the smaller, apparently weaker man of law has stood up to the tougher gunman, winning Doniphon's respect. While courage is necessary, it's not sufficient to win the fight against Liberty Valance, and if Stoddard goes up against him, he will probably be killed.

The evening of their shoot-out looks as if it will play out that way: Valance taunts Stoddard and easily shoots the gun out of his hand while townsfolk look on in dread. But Stoddard manages to retrieve his gun and apparently shoots Valance, killing him. The rest is history. As "the man who shot Liberty Valance," Stoddard will stand for senator and win the election.

Meanwhile, Doniphon, who witnessed the gunfight, watches as Hallie dresses Stoddard's wounds. He knows now that Hallie will never marry him. In a drunken rage, he sets fire to his homestead and is rescued from the flames by his black ranch hand and friend, Pompey, played by the reliable and stalwart Woody Strode. Doniphon's dreams are over. Returning to the present day, twenty-five years later, Pompey is the only other mourner at Doniphon's funeral, aside from Senator Stoddard and his wife, Hallie. Pompey reveals that Doniphon's last years were grim ones.

As in *The Searchers*, Duke Wayne's star power allows the audience to remain sympathetic to a character who loses the girl, loses his home, and loses his way, a sympathy that deepens with the suggestion that Hallie still cares for him—perhaps even loves him. But more important is the final revelation that it was Doniphon, not Stoddard, who killed Liberty Valance. In a mini flashback the scene is replayed, Doniphon standing in the shadows with his rifle, felling Valance before he can murder young Stoddard, who is out-gunned and out of his league. Thus Doniphon—Duke Wayne—is restored to the stature of heroic savior but with the added pathos that his deed went unnoticed, unheralded, unsung.

"HEROES DON'T BRAG"

The mystery is *why* Doniphon—who might have a chance to win Hallie back—never sets the record straight. He allows her to go off with Stoddard, thinking him a hero for defeating Liberty Valance. Why has Doniphon admitted defeat so easily? Why does he let his rival prevail in all things? Perhaps his sneak attack on Liberty Valance would have led to a murder trial if made public. Or per-haps he recognizes that the old ways are indeed changing and that his way—keeping order at the business end of a gun—is going the way of the stagecoach. Ford doesn't elaborate, but one thing we can be sure of is that Duke is the real hero of the picture—the hero who remains unsung—and Stoddard has to live with the knowledge that his reputation is based on a lie.

Doniphon's self-effacing decision is rooted in the heroic arche-type Ford and Wayne built together. Simply put, heroes don't brag. It would have been unsporting for Doniphon to seize Stoddard's glory, no matter the truth of the situation. His mentorship of the younger man also comes into play: at great personal cost, he's will-ing to let Stoddard take the glory that should have gone to him.

This truth isn't made public until the end of the film, when Stoddard gives an interview to a young newspaperman, describing what really happened. About to rush out to print the true story, his editor tells him not to. "When the legend becomes fact," he famously says, "print the legend."

For all of its lasting recognition, that line's meaning is not beyond dispute. Peter Bogdanovich has gone on record to say that the phrase is widely misunderstood because it's meant ironically. "It's one of the most ironic lines in the history of movies," he says. "If he had meant that, he wouldn't have made the movie! He made it very clear what the truth was" and that history is full of such moments.

Bogdanovich once asked the old master if his sympathy was with John Wayne and the Old West in *Liberty Valance* or with Stoddard, the new kind of hero. Ford's answer was typically evasive: "Well, Wayne was the central character, the motivator of the whole thing," though Stewart has more screen time. But if the hero doesn't win and the winner isn't heroic, then we have the first truly ambiguous Western—revisionist really—in which the very idea of heroism is called into question. In a sense, each of the two lead characters is half a man, and their two approaches are incomplete without the other: guns alone won't win the peace, and the law needs to be backed up by force. "It's his last word on the West. Men of law cannot succeed without the backup of force," Bogdanovich explained. "John Ford saw that in the war." It's John Ford's farewell to the myth of complete self-sufficiency backed by gun prowess—the endlessly played-out drama of who's faster on the draw in legions of mid-century Westerns. With *Liberty Valance*, Ford ushers in a period of profound change for the genre he helped create.

"It's a haunted film, haunted by the past," says film critic Richard Schickel. "John Wayne's character is lost in history. It's antimythic—that's the sadness of the movie." At the end, Doniphon is a lost soul without his beloved Hallie, without the homestead he built by hand and then destroyed, without the glory of having killed a notorious outlaw. But Stoddard at the end of the film realizes that he's a fraud, propelled to success on the back of a lie.

Even though "the hero doesn't win, the winner isn't heroic," in Ford's words, *Liberty Valance* is the director's last great Western, considered "culturally, historically, or aesthetically significant" by the Library of Congress's National Film Registry. Its revisionist view of the frontier hero, and its recognition of the end of that era, add to the complexity and ambiguity of Ford's oeuvre and to the Western genre itself.

7

Journey to Manhood:
Teaching the Next Generation

He could never forgive himself for not being superhuman.
—PILAR WAYNE

If you give me the chance, I'll do my best work.
—JOHN WAYNE

In a 2015 *New York Times* op-ed column on wolves, animal behaviorist Carl Safina described new research that showed alpha males to be a wolf pack's chief nurturers of pups, often singling out the weakest ones for special attention. He described the actions of a specific alpha male, "21"—known as a "super wolf" for his fierceness—being tracked in Yellowstone National Park. What wolf 21 seemed to enjoy most within his own family was to "wrestle with the little pups," noted Safina. "And what he really loved to do was to pretend to lose." Wolf 21 was also observed looking out for the sickliest pup in the pack and spending time with him. "Strength impresses us," he writes, "[but] kindness is what we remember best."

Safina quotes veteran wolf researcher Rick McIntyre, who observed that the main characteristic of an alpha male wolf "is a quiet confidence. . . . You lead by example." And Doug Smith, project leader for the Yellowstone Gray Wolf Restoration Project, noted that females "do most of the decision making. . . . It's the alpha female who really runs the show." But he went on to remark that "men can learn a thing or two from real wolves: less snarl, more quiet confidence, leading by example, faithful devotion in the care and defense of families, respect for females and a sharing of responsibilities."

That combination of fierceness, strength, nurturing, and looking out for the weak is well expressed in two of Duke Wayne's post-Ford pictures: *True Grit* in 1969 and *The Cowboys* in 1972. Both roles were welcome departures from the usual John Wayne image: one was comedic and self-parodying, and the other portrayed Duke as an older man forced to recognize the limits of his strength as he passes on his knowledge to a passel of boys. But this wasn't just a frank acknowledgment that his career was close to running its course. Events in Duke's off-screen life had raised the possibility that he would never act again.

THE BIG *C*

Making *The Alamo* had left him exhausted, with a phlegmatic cough that sounded eerily like his father's tubercular rasps, but he continued his five-pack-a-day cigarette habit. "His constant coughing," recalled Pilar Wayne, "reawakened childhood memories of hearing his tubercular father cough in the stillness of a desert night. To be ill was torture for such a physical man. To have the illness remind him of such an unhappy period of his life seemed doubly cruel."

He was filming *In Harm's Way* with Patricia Neal on location in Hawaii in 1964 when his coughing got so bad it interrupted filming. Duke kept insisting that everything was fine, but he went willingly to Scripps Clinic in La Jolla, California, with Pilar at his side; to ease his mind, she had agreed to take all the same tests he was undergoing. An X-ray revealed a spot on Duke's left lung.

"I knew Duke was very sick," she wrote in her memoir. He tried to make light of the results, telling her that the doctor "thinks it's just valley fever." Pilar recalled, "Duke was a terrible liar. Choking back tears, I said, 'What are they going to do?' His voice was a hoarse monotone as he answered, 'I'm scheduled for exploratory surgery in a few days, at Good Samaritan Hospital.'"

She acknowledged that "neither of us was able to say the word 'cancer' because, back in 1964, a diagnosis of lung cancer was a virtual death sentence." Not only that, Duke's agent, Charlie Feldman, warned Duke that "you'll never work again once the studios hear you've got cancer." That was the real death sentence: Duke loved his family, but he lived to work. Pilar saw that "Duke wasn't sure he'd want to go on living if he couldn't go on working. . . . He could live without the lung if he had to, but he couldn't live without his work." Professionally, he already felt trapped in the role of an undefeatable hero; if he survived the cancer, how could he live up to that daunting straitjacket of an image? As an act of rebellion, Duke began smoking even more heavily.

Two weeks later, on September 17, Duke underwent a six-hour operation at Good Samaritan Hospital in Los Angeles, where a cancerous tumor the size of a golf ball was excised from his left lung. The surgeon had to remove two of Duke's ribs as well as the upper lobe of his lung, leaving him dependent on the remaining right lung. To make matters worse, his stitches ripped open after a bout of intense coughing, his face and body swelled with edema, and he had to undergo a second surgery five days later, landing him in intensive care.

Though his cancer had been removed, Duke was deeply depressed over his diagnosis and the possibility that he would no longer be able to support Pilar and their two young children, Aissa, then eight, and Ethan, two. And there was the added strain of trying to keep the cancer diagnosis from the reporters who hung around the hospital, trying to suss out the truth about Duke's condition. He also wanted to keep the news from John Ford, who, at seventy, was in poor health himself and was disappointed over the failure of *Donovan's Reef*, the final picture he had made with Duke, which was practically booed out of theaters the year before. He had intended this film to be one last rollicking comedy, a final tribute to male camaraderie and to his old commanding officer during World War II, "Wild" Bill Donovan, but in retrospect everything about it seemed an exercise in obsolescence. When Ford got word about Duke's condition, he shook off his malaise and immediately flew in from Hawaii to visit Duke in the hospital.

"He is like a son to me," Duke's old mentor—and tormentor—confided to Pilar, but Pilar felt his underlying sadness, his resignation to the fact that the glory days of the Ford stock acting company—and the great pictures that Duke had made with Pappy—were behind them. What neither Pilar nor Ford could know was that Duke still had a few great pictures in him, including one that would finally bring him an Academy Award.

TRUE GRIT

In an early scene in *True Grit*, released in 1969, produced by Hal B. Wallis and directed by Henry Hathaway, the good people of an Arkansas town are singing "Amazing Grace" as they watch a public hanging of three hapless miscreants. It's a scene that could have been staged by John Ford, except that the beloved gospel is used as the backdrop of a grim scene rather than to celebrate the virtues of community.

Duke read the galleys of *True Grit*, Charles Portis's lively 1968 novel, and knew immediately that U.S. marshal Rooster Cogburn was a role he could inhabit. The irascible, over-the-hill, heavy-drinking, one-eyed marshal seemed to combine the most salient traits of John Ford and John Wayne, even allowing Duke to wear a black eye patch like his hero and mentor and use his age and bulky weight to his advantage. Even better, it had a comic dimension that gave him a chance to make fun of his macho image, now set in bronze and increasingly burdensome as he grew too old, and too ill, to live up to the demanding responsibilities of "being

John Wayne." Instead, Duke relished playing a Falstaffian figure—
blustery, comic, fat—but one with undisputed courage who still
possesses the skill, when needed, to take down an outlaw gang.

Through Batjac, he made an offer to Portis to buy the film
rights for $300,000, but he was too late; producer Hal Wallis had
already snapped them up and had hired another tough-guy director, Henry Hathaway, with whom Duke had worked on five previous films, beginning with *The Shepherd of the Hills* in 1941.

At sixty-one, Duke was arguably too old for the role of Rooster
Cogburn, a fortyish U.S. marshal, so Charles Portis didn't think
John Wayne was right for the part. But Duke really wanted it.
Not only did he admire Portis's novel, but he was blown away by
Marguerite Roberts's script—which preserves much of the novel's
saucy dialogue—considering it the best screenplay he had ever
read. One of the pleasures of Portis's novel is his use of the poetic
rhythms and parable-heavy language of the King James Bible, adding an authentic, nineteenth-century feel to the dialogue. "I won't
put a thief into my mouth to steal my wits," young Mattie Ross,
played by Kim Darby, tells Rooster Cogburn when he offers her
a drink. When Mattie explains why it has fallen to her to hire
Cogburn to avenge her father's murder, she says, "My mother's
indecisive and hobbled by grief."

Born in Colorado, Roberts liked writing scenes for tough guys.
"I was weaned on stories about gunfighters and their doings," she
said, "and I know all the lingo, too. My grandfather came West as
far as Colorado by covered wagon. He was a sheriff in the state's
wildest days." "There was a kind of beauty that was different from
most Westerns," Wayne later said. "My part was as beautifully
written a thing as I've ever read. And the girl's part was the best
part I ever read in my whole life." Luckily for Duke, Hal Wallis
and Henry Hathaway both wanted him in the role, and they signed
him.

It was ironic, perhaps, given Duke's outspoken conservative
politics, that he fell so in love with Marguerite Roberts's screenplay. After a lucrative career as a screenwriter in the 1930s, she

had been blacklisted when she and her husband, the writer John Sanford, who was briefly a member of the Communist Party, had refused to testify before the House Un-American Activities Committee. Not only did Duke put aside his right-wing views, but he made sure the screenplay was accepted and billed under her name.

True Grit's mix of adventure, drama, and comedy would prove irresistible to the public, right down to the pairing of a tough, cranky old coot, Marshal Reuben J. "Rooster" Cogburn, with Mattie Ross, a feisty fourteen-year-old girl who comes to town from her family's farm in Yell County, Arkansas, to track down her father's killer. She proves to be Cogburn's match in many ways, exhibiting as much courage, savvy, and persistence as the seasoned pursuer of miscreants, who spends his off time drinking corn whiskey on a broken-down daybed in a Chinese immigrant's dingy store, shooting rats with his Peacemaker.

Mattie hires Rooster Cogburn, the toughest U.S. marshal in the land, who, she believes, has "true grit," to go after Tom Chaney, the man who gunned down her father. "I won't rest until Tom Chaney is barking in hell!" she tells Cogburn. Chaney, played with whiny self-pity by the veteran actor Jeff Corey, has hightailed it out to Indian Territory to join up with "Lucky" Ned Pepper's gang of outlaws, beyond the arm of the law but within the boundary-crossing grasp of Marshal Cogburn. A young Robert Duvall plays Ned Pepper, and Dennis Hopper plays Moon, one of the unfortunate, but oddly eloquent, members of Ned Pepper's gang. In his final scene, as he lies dying on the dirt floor of a dugout where the Pepper gang is about to rendezvous, Moon says with his last breath, "I am bleeding buckets! I am gone. Send the news to my brother, George Garrett. He is a Methodist circuit rider in South Texas. You can write care of the district supervisor in Austin. . . . I will meet him later walking the streets of Glory!"

True Grit's cast is all the more remarkable considering who passed on various roles. Elvis Presley—Elvis Presley!—was offered the role of a bumptious Texas Ranger named La Boeuf, who has been on Chaney's trail for some time; Chaney has a price on his

*

Duke as the Falstaffian Rooster Cogburn, with Kim Darby
as Mattie, in *True Grit*, 1969. Duke manages to send up his
own image, with a nod toward Ford by donning an eye patch.

head for the murder of a Texas senator, so La Boeuf joins forces with Cogburn and Mattie, against Mattie's wishes. But Elvis Presley's agent demanded that he be given top billing over John Wayne, and because that wasn't going to happen, the part went to a newcomer to the movie business, one of the most popular country-western singers of the day, Glen Campbell. Hathaway, however, resented that bit of casting, feeling it was done just to guarantee a hit for the movie's title song. Composed by Elmer Bernstein with lyrics by Don Black, "True Grit" was indeed nominated for the Golden Globe and the Academy Award for Best Song.

For the bold and strong-minded role of Mattie Ross, Mia Farrow was the director's first choice, until Robert Mitchum, who had just worked with the actress in *Secret Ceremony*, convinced Farrow that Henry Hathaway would prove too ornery a director for her. Duke suggested another singer with no acting experience—the tragic Karen Carpenter, an early sufferer of anorexia—and he even wanted his daughter Aissa to be considered for the part, but Wallis rejected those ideas. The role was then offered to two delicate blondes, Tuesday Weld and Sondra Locke, both of whom turned it down. So a relative unknown, Kim Darby, was cast as Mattie, and her tomboyish appearance and unswerving gaze suited her well for the part of the girl from Yell County who won't take no for an answer and who can bully Marshal Cogburn into doing her bidding. Her weapons? Besides the clumsy, misfiring Colt Dragoon left to her by her murdered father, she has native wit, a sharp tongue, courage, and unstoppable resolve. In short, she has true grit, the quality she most admires. "My God, she reminds me of me," Rooster Cogburn exclaims after Mattie crosses a river on the back of her Texas pony, Little Blackie, so as not to be left behind.

If Mattie is equal to Marshal Cogburn in the possession of grit—and she is—does Cogburn mentor her? After all, she provides the funds, the motive, and the resolve to go after her prey, and she proves herself an able companion on the trail. Indeed, she already has a grown-up mind and a formed character, and she doesn't need

✻

Duke won his only Academy Award for *True Grit*.

nurturing. In truth, Cogburn—though decades older in years and experience—doesn't mentor her as much as he *protects* her, even to the point of going to extreme measures to save her life.

After initially siding with La Boeuf against Mattie, whom they both consider a liability on the trail of a killer, Cogburn swings around to her side against the interloping Texas Ranger. The turning point arrives when La Boeuf spanks Mattie for her insolence and to punish her for tagging along, and Cogburn stops the Texas Ranger, pointing out that he's enjoying it too much. At that point, any paternal instincts Cogburn has left in him after the disintegration of his own family years earlier, including the loss of a son, kick in. From then on, the cranky old marshal will continue to squabble with Mattie but will keep an eye out to protect her, not just from La Boeuf, but from Ned Pepper's gang.

In the climactic scene, after Mattie falls into a pit of rattlesnakes and is bitten by one of them, Rooster Cogburn takes her onto the back of her stalwart pony and rides day and night until the pony collapses under them. But they do reach an Indian doctor who saves her life, though in the novel, and in the 2010 remake by Joel and Ethan Coen, her arm is amputated.

In the movie's final scene, Cogburn visits Mattie on her family's farm in Yell County, where Mattie has laid out a place for him in the Ross family graveyard. He has *become* her family—a father figure to a fatherless girl—and in a final recognition of both his obsolescence as a cowboy hero and his tough endurance, he jumps his horse over a four-rail fence and tells Mattie to "come and see a fat man ride." Against all odds and his own encroaching decrepitude, not only has he triumphed in wiping out the outlaw Ned Pepper's gang and in bringing about the death of Tom Chaney— shot by a dying La Boeuf to save Mattie's and Cogburn's lives— but, more important, he has endured.

It was a triumphant role, and for the first time in a career spanning five decades, John Wayne won the Academy Award for Best Actor, beating out such competition as Richard Burton for *Anne of the Thousand Days.* "Wow! If I'd known what I know now, I'd have put a patch on my eye thirty-five years ago," Duke famously said.

In 2011, the great Western novelist Larry McMurtry teamed up with his screen-writing partner Diana Ossana, with whom he co-wrote *Brokeback Mountain,* to talk about Henry Hathaway's 1969 *True Grit* and the Coen brothers' remake, which starred Jeff Bridges in Duke's role, Matt Damon as La Boeuf, Hailee Steinfeld as Mattie Ross, and Josh Brolin as Tom Chaney. They concluded that "the story of *True Grit* is mainly a study of loyalty. Reluctant loyalty, it is true, but loyalty nonetheless." There's no clearer assertion that the idea of the reluctant hero, introduced in *Stagecoach,* has come full circle thirty years later. Rooster Cogburn acknowledges this himself, in his own colorful way: "I'm a foolish old man who's been drawn into a wild goose chase by a harpy in trousers and a nincompoop."

THE COWBOYS

The Cowboys, a 1972 Warner Bros. Western directed by Mark Rydell, was made three years after *True Grit.* Again, Duke lobbied for the role of Wil Andersen, an aging rancher whose cowhands have deserted him to chase a gold rush, forcing him to recruit and train the only help he can find for a four-hundred-mile cattle drive—a handful of schoolboys. George C. Scott was Rydell's first choice, and he was reluctant to cast Wayne because of their radically different politics and his doubts about Duke's health. Rydell, a onetime actor from the Bronx who had come up through the Actors Studio in New York, described himself as a liberal, and he was leery of Duke's right-wing views; it was only four years after John Wayne's polemical *The Green Berets,* which forcefully argued for America's continued involvement in Vietnam. But Rydell met with Duke in Durango, Mexico, where the actor was filming *Big Jake,* a Batjac production under the helm of his son Michael.

Rydell was surprised by Duke's humility and his eagerness to take on the role. "The political John Wayne never showed up," recalled Roscoe Lee Browne, who played Jebediah Nightlinger, the eloquent and loquacious trail cook in *The Cowboys*. As if he were a novice actor, Duke asked Rydell for the part by saying, "If you give me the chance, I'll do my best work."

"He *wanted* it," Rydell recalled later, and despite his initial misgivings he never regretted the chance to work with the Hollywood legend. However, he did rather relish the fact that Sarah Cunningham, the actress who played Annie, Wil Andersen's wife, had been blacklisted by Hollywood, a practice Duke had tacitly supported. This was her first role since being blacklisted in 1955, but if Duke had any idea about her past, he didn't let on. Or perhaps, just as he had championed Marguerite Roberts's screenplay adaptation of *True Grit*, he knew now to keep his politics out of his working life.

In addition to Sarah Cunningham and Roscoe Lee Browne, Rydell surrounded Duke with a cast of superb, Actors Studio–trained actors, including Bruce Dern as the magnificently weaselly villain and ex-con Asa Watts, who tries to steal Andersen's herd after being turned down as a cowhand; and Colleen Dewhurst as a warm and earthy madam, corralling a wagonload of impossibly blond and beautiful young prostitutes, with whom at least one man on the cattle drive—the trail cook Nightlinger—will find pleasure. Nightlinger makes it clear, though, that the women are off-limits to the boys. Added to this stellar, mostly East Coast roster of actors was an old Hollywood friend of Duke's, the folksy character actor Slim Pickens.

Duke felt challenged by the Method-trained actors. As in *The Big Trail*, when he was a neophyte set among theatrically trained easterners, and in *Red River*, when he played opposite Monty Clift, one of the greatest Method actors to come out of the Actors Studio, Duke knew he had to hold his own against performers with different, and deeper, training than his on-the-job Hollywood-star school of acting. But he rose to the occasion. "He loved being pushed, he loved being challenged," Rydell remembered. He was won over by Duke's cooperation and work ethic. "John Wayne was a very impressive figure," he later said. "He had solidity, power, commitment. He was determined to act brilliantly in the picture . . . he was challenged by the actors who surrounded him. He didn't have that training, but he was to be as good as the best of them."

Rydell also noticed that Duke was far more sensitive and erudite than his image would have one believe. He once overheard Duke and Roscoe Lee Browne—a Shakespearean actor and poet as well as a product of the Actors Studio—exchanging quotations from poems by Shelley and Keats. Ultimately, according to Rydell, Duke "felt he raised his acting level ten times to work with Studio-trained actors."

But at one point during production, Rydell yelled at Duke, embarrassing him in front of the entire cast and crew, when Duke rode too soon into a difficult scene that had been set up involving hundreds of cattle. Rydell later fretted that he would be fired for his outburst. But Duke invited him to dinner and told him that he had reminded him of Ford. "Jack Ford treated me like that," he reassured his director, who was just forty-two at the time. From that point on, Duke called the younger man "sir" and made it clear that he considered the director his boss, worthy of respect. "I was very touched and impressed by that," recalled Rydell.

※

After being deserted by his former cowhands, Duke's Wil Andersen describes his dilemma to his friend Anse, played by the former rodeo cowboy Slim Pickens. What can he do when there are no men left to drive his cattle to market? Anse reminds Wil that he himself had made his first cattle drive at the age of thirteen, so Wil goes to the only place left to find cowboys who can possibly do the job—a one-room schoolhouse where he will recruit schoolboys for the drive. One of the first things he tells the boys, who range in age from nine to fifteen, is "I'm a man and you're boys," emphasizing that they will be cow*boys*, taking their orders from him.

Of the eleven actors hired to play the recruited cowboys, six were what Rydell described as "country boys" who had already been in rodeos. The rest were actors who had to learn how to ride and rope, just as the rodeo boys had to learn how to act—a more difficult task, Rydell noted. A few of the standouts were Robert Carradine, who played Slim Honeycutt, the most senior of the schoolhouse group at fifteen; Sean Kelly as Stuttering Bob; Clay O'Brien Cooper as Hardy Fimps, one of the "country boys" who would grow up to earn seven rodeo world championships; Mike Pyeatt as the frightened Homer Weems, who is terrorized by the predator Asa Watts; and A. Martinez as an older boy called Cimarron.

Cimarron is the most troubled and the most interesting of the crew of young cowboys, the only one not recruited from the prairie schoolhouse. Part Native American, rejected by both white and Indian society, he calls himself "a mistake of nature," yet he already has the appearance and self-possession of a young man. An eternal outsider, Cimarron seethes with anger and resentment, threatening to destabilize the group of would-be wranglers and posing a threat to Andersen's authority. Though he outrides and outropes the rest of the boys, he is summarily rejected after instigating a knock-down, drag-out fight with Slim. Later he will be allowed back into the fold and—through Andersen's belief in him—will learn to harness his temper and master himself.

In an era when boys *wanted* to grow up and become men, Rydell recalled, the young actors were "thrilled to have the opportunity to appear alongside John Wayne," who was often the favorite actor of their fathers and even grandfathers. One of the boys, the future rodeo star Clay O'Brien Cooper, said that John Wayne up there on his horse seemed to have "an aura around him, a kind of white light."

What must have surprised them was the degree to which the most famous Hollywood actor of their day genuinely looked after the boys, mentoring them, just as his character, Wil Andersen, mentors his young posse throughout the picture. Duke would later describe taking on that role as "the greatest experience of my life." Nurturing and teaching the young were important to him, in life and in art, and he was concerned about and protective of the young cast. "He was very paternal and very loving," said Rydell. "Wayne didn't pull back. He loved being a father, and he was a father to [those] boys . . . he loved it."

After he is stalked, robbed, beaten, and shot in the back by Watts, Wil Andersen's dying words to the young boys he's trained who will now carry on without him are "Every man wants his children to be better than he was. You are. I'm proud of you"—words so many sons and daughters long to hear from their fathers and, too often, do not. Having already buried his own two sons, who are revealed to have been a disappointment to him, Andersen gets a second chance at fatherhood by mentoring these eleven boys. When he is laid to rest on a lonely mesa, his epitaph reads,

WIL ANDERSEN
BELOVED HUSBAND
AND FATHER

Just as Rooster Cogburn is given a second chance to be a protective father to Mattie Ross in *True Grit*, so is Wil Andersen given that second chance, taking on the education of eleven boys who would be men.

✳

Rydell filmed mostly on location in Colorado and New Mexico, and at one point John Ford made a visit to the shoot. Rydell was honored—"Anyone who's ever directed knows how great he is"—and he noticed that Duke "followed him around like a pussycat. It was a wonderful thing to watch." Ford witnessed the crucial scene in which Asa Watts battles it out with Andersen, shooting him several times in the back after a long and brutal fight. Ford was impressed with the scene, though Bruce Dern—terrifying

even in real life, frightening the young actors with his intensity—
would find it hard to get work for a while after being known as the
man who killed John Wayne. No one could believe that a hero of
Wayne's stature could be killed by such a sniveling villain. "America will hate you for this," Duke reportedly warned his co-star, to
which Bruce Dern replied, "Yeah, but they'll love me in Berkeley."

As much as he loved the experience and the role of Wil Andersen, it was a physically demanding shoot. Duke did many of his
own stunts, as he had in *True Grit*, regardless of his compromised
physical condition after the cancer operation. "It was hard on him,"
Rydell said, and at the time he wasn't aware that he was endanger-
ing his lead actor, who had trouble breathing at twelve thousand
feet above sea level. Staging the brutal fight with Bruce Dern was
particularly difficult, and it took two days to film.

Critical reception of *The Cowboys* was mixed. It was risky in
the 1970s to show the death of a child—one of the cowboys is
trampled to death—especially as the Vietnam War still raged. A
number of critics complained that the film endorsed youth violence
when the cowboys avenge Andersen's death by outwitting and
slaying Asa Watts and his cattle rustlers—all seventeen of them.
Pauline Kael wrote scathingly in *The New Yorker*, "One could easily think that Warner Bros. and the director . . . were in the business of corrupting minors, because this movie is about how these
schoolboys become men through learning the old-fashioned virtues of killing." She's particularly critical of "the way that people
don't die in clean kills but writhe in slow torture." Yet, as Rydell
has pointed out, *The Cowboys* was far less violent than Sam Peckinpah's *Wild Bunch*, released only a week after *True Grit* three
years earlier. Peckinpah sought to depict violent gunplay in a more
realistic fashion than previous Westerns had; he also intended the
bloodbaths to be cathartic to an audience numbed by television
images of the Vietnam War. But audiences seemed to relish the
violence in *The Wild Bunch* rather than find it horrifying, a fact
that troubled him greatly. The bloody ballet of Peckinpah's ode

✳

In 1972's *The Cowboys*, Wayne was as protective of his
young fellow actors off camera as he was on-screen.

to the end of the independent-gunfighter era makes *The Cowboys* worthy of its PG-rated, family-friendly status by comparison.

When asked if his movie promoted vigilantism, Rydell answered, "The picture has a legendary quality. . . . It's not topical; it's about what it means to be a man and take responsibility for your actions." He asserted that it was a heroic thing to avenge a father's death and reclaim the stolen herd, especially at a time and in a place where there are "no police on the frontier." "What can we do?" the boys ask Nightlinger after they're stranded by Asa's gang. "We can be men," Roscoe answers, which has an added punch because, as the only black character in the movie, his mantle of full manhood has been particularly hard won—a fact dramatized in the film when Asa and his gang try, unsuccessfully, to lynch him.

There is one scene, however, that demonstrates an element of unintended cruelty. Wil Andersen berates Stuttering Bob when his stutter prevents him from calling for help when Slim Honeycutt nearly drowns. Andersen harshly blames the boy for Slim's brush with death, criticizing him incessantly while the boy tries to brand Andersen "a son of a bitch" until—miraculously—the stutter vanishes. It's a cringe-inducing moment in the picture, a scene in which Andersen shows himself to be a bully whose behavior would, in reality, likely have worsened the boy's condition. Tough love always works in the movies but often misfires horrifically in real life.

Yet there is a grace note to the relentless urging of young boys to get up before dawn—"we're burning daylight!"—ride and rope relentlessly throughout the day, and ultimately act like men. When Andersen sends the terrified Homer Weems to stand watch at night, not knowing that he has already been terrorized by Watts, Nightlinger questions Andersen's judgment. In response, Andersen offers a kind of apology. "You think I was too rough on the boy?" he asks. "I can't say I always decide right." This Duke Wayne can admit he might be wrong, which is another important part of learning what it means to become a man.

Rydell, his disapproval of Duke's right-wing political stance firmly in the rear-view mirror, came to respect and admire the aging actor. "Wayne loved the script and didn't change anything. He was a great collaborator. . . . He was the sweetest man."

Four years later, Duke would have one more chance to play a similar role on-screen, in his final film, *The Shootist*.

8

Going West: Twilight of the Gods

I have a lust for . . . dignity.
—JOHN WAYNE

FINAL DAYS AND FAREWELLS

Liberty Valance was Ford's last great Western, but it wasn't his final turn at directing cowboys. He followed *Valance* up with *How the West Was Won*, a 1963 historical saga of western conquest he co-directed with George Marshall and Henry Hathaway, and the following year he co-produced and directed his last Western, *Cheyenne Autumn*, a sympathetic and thus revisionist depiction of the Cheyenne people and their mistreatment by the U.S. Bureau of Indian Affairs. "I've long wanted to do a story that tells the truth about them and not just a picture in which they're chased by the cavalry," he said. "I've killed more Indians than Custer. This is their side."

But filming dragged on and on, well behind schedule, unusual for a John Ford movie, until Warner Bros. ordered him off the shoot. That plunged Ford into a fit of pique. He began drinking, something he never used to do while making a movie. Ben Johnson, whom he'd finally hired again after an eleven-year hiatus, said, "That's when the whole thing fell apart. They sent another director up there to finish the job."

Ford, who turned seventy in 1964, was just worn out. His penultimate film, 1965's *Young Cassidy*, about the life of Irish playwright Sean O'Casey, brought him back to his beloved Ireland, yet even there he did not return to form. He was pleased to return to Dublin to work on the film starring Rod Taylor, Julie Christie, and Maggie Smith, but *Cheyenne Autumn* seemed to have permanently broken his resolve never to drink while directing. Michael Killanin, Ford's Irish friend and co-producer on *The Quiet Man* and *Young Cassidy*, spent time with Ford on location in Dublin and discovered bottles of Scotch stashed in Ford's living quarters. Weakened by a bout of strep throat, drinking heavily, Ford returned to California, and the film was completed by his cinematographer, the distinguished Jack Cardiff. He nursed his desolation aboard the *Araner*, embittered by the lackluster reception of his recent films, his ill health, and his dwindling clout in the motion picture business. By this time he walked with a limp and was so hard of hearing that people had to shout to be heard. His marriage had finally deteriorated, with Mary talking about a separation, and the two of them occupying distant rooms of their house. And his contentious relationship with his only son, Patrick, who had worked with him on so many films, finally came to a breaking point. Ford was outraged when, in 1965, Pat asked him for money after the birth of his daughter, and the two never really spoke again. The poor reception of *Cheyenne Autumn* further dispirited him, and he sulked among the mementos and relics of his once illustrious and deeply satisfying career: a war bonnet from the Battle of Little Bighorn, Buffalo Bill Cody's gloves, a black silver-mounted saddle.

Ford made his last picture, *7 Women*, with MGM in 1966, and he viewed it as another way to rejuvenate his career, and perhaps a chance to be reunited with Kate Hepburn. This film celebrating the heroism of nurses captured in World War II was his only effort with a nearly all-woman cast. However, Hepburn was unavailable and Patricia Neal took her part, until she was felled by a devastating stroke while making the film and was replaced by Anne Bancroft. But Ford was tired, and he lost interest in the picture, telling his brother-in-law and co-producer, Bernard Smith, "Let's do the goddamn thing. It's no good, but let's do it and get the hell out."

After the poor reception of *7 Women*, Ford stopped getting offers to work. He flew to Honolulu to lick his wounds, depressed and often drunk. Back home in Bel Air, he holed up in his bedroom, where he drank, watched TV, and read. News of Duke Wayne's lung cancer, diagnosed in 1964, stunned him, and he visited his former mentee at Good Samaritan Hospital, reliving the good old days with Pilar.

In 1971, Ford was diagnosed with inoperable abdominal cancer. Facing up to the bitter news, Jack and Mary Ford sold their home in Los Angeles and moved to a five-bedroom Spanish-style house on Old Prospector Trail in Palm Desert so he could be closer to the Eisenhower Hospital, where he would undergo treatment. As before, the two resided in opposite wings, though they became closer in the final months of Ford's life. Filmdom showered honors on his illustrious career, such as the Venice Film Festival's Golden Lion Award and the Life Achievement Award from the American Film Institute, while at the same time continuing to make the kinds of movies that Jack Ford hated, with graphic sex scenes that he particularly loathed. "I don't like porn," he announced when asked if he'd seen *Midnight Cowboy*. "These easy, liberal movies. A lot of junk. I don't know where they're going. They don't either"— this from a man who had once been considered a social Democrat. Acclaim came from beyond the film industry; President Nixon awarded him the Presidential Medal of Freedom, an honor he felt paled beside being made a rear admiral in the U.S. Navy, the institution he loved far more than Hollywood.

But the end had finally come for old Jack Ford. Fighting cancer, weak and emaciated, Ford received a string of friends in the final three weeks of his life who had come by to say their farewells. Director William Wyler and veteran film editor Robert Parrish, who had been a member of Ford's Field Photographic Branch, came, as did Peter Bogdanovich and Kate Hepburn. Bogdanovich was shocked at how gaunt and old Ford looked. Ben Johnson, lately restored to the Old Man's graces, came to his deathbed, and Howard Hawks—Ford's good friend, who lived in Palm Desert and who had shown him what John Wayne was capable of in *Red River*—visited often.

Ford asked to see Duke, who rushed to his side. Losing Ford was like losing his father all over again—a much tougher, meaner, yet idealized father at whose hands Duke had both suffered and prospered. Yet when he arrived, Ford sarcastically said, "Come for the death watch, Duke?"

If he was taken aback by that gruff question, he didn't show it. He was used to navigating Jack Ford's roughness. "Hell, no. You're the anchor. You'll bury us all," Duke reportedly answered.

When Kate Hepburn arrived, Dan Ford, the director's grandson, had a tape recorder on hand to capture the Old Man's last words. Instead, Dan recorded his grandfather's conversation with Hepburn as she sat with him and reminisced. At one point Ford apparently asked Dan to turn off the recorder while he spoke privately with the actress he so greatly admired, but it stayed on, recording their last words together. Ford's voice unmistakably says to Hepburn, "I love you," a shocking utterance from the gruff, tormented man who had relegated the majority of his sentiment to his moving pictures.

Curiously, it was Woody Strode who remained with Ford for his final six hours as the old director slipped into a coma and passed away at 6:00 p.m. on August 31, 1973. Barbara was nursing her father at the end because Mary, crippled by Parkinson's at that point, was too incapacitated. Strode later described how he and Barbara draped an American flag over Ford's body and toasted him with two glasses of brandy, which they then tossed into the fireplace, shattering them.

A few days after Ford's death, Kate Hepburn was interviewed at length on *The Dick Cavett Show*. She talked about how Jack Ford had given Spencer Tracy his start in the movies and what a canny director he was, though life had been hard for him. "He was Irish," she said, "and the Irish have such great imaginations that it's hard for them to live in the world." Hepburn concluded, "Jack Ford died like [a] gentlem[a]n, with great courage."

"FEO, FUERTE Y FORMAL"

Spanish for "ugly, strong, and dignified," this is the motto Duke wanted engraved as his epitaph, and it well describes John Bernard Books, the dying gunman Duke played in his final film, *The Shootist*, made in 1976, three years before his own death from cancer. Based on the legendary Texas gunman John Wesley Hardin, who once shot a man for snoring, from a novel by the popular Western writer Glendon Swarthout, it co-starred Lauren Bacall and Ron Howard and was directed by Don Siegel, best known for the classic 1956 sci-fi movie *Invasion of the Body Snatchers* and for five Clint Eastwood films, including *Dirty Harry* and *Escape from Alcatraz*.

Swarthout found the term "shootist" in a newspaper clipping from the 1880s that used the word to describe men who lived by the gun, a synonym for "gunman," "man killer," and "assassin." Books is identified as "the most legendary shootist extant" at the outset of the film, and a killer of thirty men, and his iconic status is established by a montage of clips from earlier John Wayne Westerns, showing the actor in all his tough, virile beauty in shoot-outs with various outlaws. There are few actors whose body of work could have been used so well to establish the character's backstory, and because it happened to be Duke's final film, it's a fitting evocation of his long, consistent, and iconic career.

The screenwriter Miles Swarthout, who adapted his father's novel for the motion picture, noted,

> As soon as Wayne had the lead, I got the idea of using clips from Big John's earlier Westerns as a unique way of quickly establishing this character's gunfighting younger days, his

violent past. . . . Look for a little piece of *Red River* (1948) to
kick off the action, followed by slices from the classics *Hondo*
(1953), *Rio Bravo* (1959), and *El Dorado* (1967).

An innovative technique at the time, it has seldom been used since
then to such good effect.

If John Wayne could have chosen a visual record of his life, his
philosophy, his cause and manner of dying, it would be *The Shootist*, and indeed Duke did choose it, because he had to lobby for the
part. "It's the kind of picture you wait for," he said. "They don't
come by often."

George C. Scott was the producers' first choice, but when
Duke read the novel, he knew it was the film he *had* to do; it would
be his sixty-ninth Western in a career of nearly two hundred films.
By 1976, John Wayne's box office clout had diminished, in part
due to a poor choice of roles since *True Grit*. He also had to per-
suade the producers, Mike Frankovich and William Self, that he
still had the stamina to undertake the role. His battle with lung
cancer had left him weakened and short of breath, looking every
bit of his sixty-nine years. He was paunchy, though still graceful
and light on his feet, and his features had coarsened. Gone was
the chiseled, Scotch-Irish beauty of his youth, but Duke managed
to lose ten pounds before filming began on location in Nevada on
January 8, 1976. Even so, Swarthout claimed that the producers
had to pay a doctor under the table to allow the actor to pass
the insurance physical. Duke grew a mustache for the part, which
further distances him from the familiar image of John Wayne but
well suits the character of a dying, apparently over-the-hill gunman. It would prove to be not only his last film role but one of his
deepest, most powerful, and most poignant.

Once the producers decided to go with Duke Wayne, other
actors of his stature asked to be in the picture as well: Duke's
friends Jimmy Stewart, Lauren Bacall, John Carradine, and Richard Boone. It's a testament to Duke's likability that an outspo-

ken, left-leaning actress like Bacall considered Duke a dear and lifelong friend, in spite of being on opposite ends of the political spectrum. Hugh O'Brian, of TV's *Wyatt Earp* fame, offered to waive his salary just to be in the movie with Duke, so he was cast in a role expanded to accommodate him: that of Jack Pulford, a cold-blooded gambler and expert with a gun. Stewart and Bacall accepted $50,000 for their roles, far less than their usual salaries, and Duke was paid his usual fee, now up to $750,000.

Having had cancer was a source of shame for Duke, a fact he'd tried to keep hidden from the studios and from his legions of fans. But in his role as the old gunslinger, he understood well Books's dour acceptance of Doc Hostetler's fatal cancer diagnosis—"You have a cancer. Advanced." It is this illness that brings Books to the bustling little town of Carson City, Nevada. The straight-shooting doctor is played by Jimmy Stewart, who, as in *Liberty Valance*, completely holds his own against his powerful co-star, though he has little screen time in a movie that belongs entirely to Duke Wayne.

In an interview on the making of *The Shootist*, Miles Swarthout recalled how his father had read an article about long-distance truckers being prone to prostate cancer, comparing them to the cowboys of the nineteenth century who spent so much of their lives in the saddle. Without a cure, Swarthout said, those men would have died a painful death. Though Books's cancer isn't described as such, the "pain like sin" deep in his spine was probably intended to be advanced prostate cancer; in any case, Doc Hostetler—at Books's insistence—reluctantly describes the progress of the disease in unembellished terms: "There will be an increase in the level of pain in your lower back, your hip, your spine. . . . The pain will become unbearable. No drug will moderate it. If you're lucky, you'll lose consciousness. Until then, you'll scream."

Indeed, for Duke to lobby for the role of a man dying of cancer, after having felt deep shame and anger over his own struggle, meant that he knew it was important to face up to the truth of the disease and to his own mortality, to lead the way in public acceptance of a disease still whispered about and euphemistically referred to as "the Big C."

The film is a profile in the courage to face up to one's end, no matter how grim. "Even an ox dies," Doc Hostetler tells Books, after first reassuring him that he seemed to have the constitution of an ox. At one point in the film when he's arguing with the widow Bond Rogers, played by Bacall, who owns the boarding-house where Books has come to die, he says to her, "I'm a dying man, scared of the dark." Those are stark, powerful words for a man celebrated for his courage and heroism.

To alleviate the pain as it grows in intensity, Hostetler gives Books a bottle of laudanum mixed with alcohol—Soldier's Joy, in fact, though the term is not used in the film—which Books then keeps in his breast pocket, taking long pulls from the bottle with increasing frequency. The doctor has pretty much warned Books that if he has any other way of going out before being beaten by the extreme pain and indignity of the disease, he ought to consider it. "Both of us have had a lot to do with death," he tells the shootist. "I'm not a brave man, but you must be. . . . I would not die the death I just described, not if I had your courage." He suggests that Books reflect on this while his mind is still clear.

Throughout the movie, Books understands that dying with dignity—as well as dignity itself—is the final virtue worth fight-ing for. He struggles for it—enduring the insults of raffish men such as the surly hothead Jay Cobb, played by Bill McKinney, and reduced to carrying a fancy red pillow stolen from a whorehouse with him wherever he goes, to relieve the pain of sitting. Early on, he cites his own moral code: "I won't be wronged, I won't be insulted, I won't be laid a hand on. I don't do that to others, and I require the same from them." But this new challenge is beyond anything Books has ever faced before. It can't be solved with a gun—or can it?

Books arrives in Carson City in 1901, a change from the nov-el's setting of El Paso, Texas, which is where the historical John

Wesley Hardin met his death in 1895 in a shoot-out in the Acme Saloon. The town bustles with modernity: A streetcar pulled by a mule runs through town on steel tracks. One of the villains of the piece, a composite character named Mike Sweeney played by a briny Richard Boone, shows up in an automobile—the Oldsmobile Curved Dash. The boardinghouse that Books moves into has a telephone, running water, and an indoor bathroom. When he comes to the boardinghouse to urge the notorious gunfighter to leave town, the local marshal, Walter Thibido, played by Harry Morgan, tells Books, "Books, it's nineteen-ought-one and the old days are over. . . . We'll have our streetcar electrified next year. . . . You plain outlived your time."

To underline the sense of an era's end, the death of Queen Victoria is announced in the local newspaper the day Books arrives: "The Queen Is Dead. Long Live the King." Books is a relic, and he has indeed outlived his time, just as the defeat of *The Alamo* for Best Picture by Billy Wilder's *The Apartment* fifteen years earlier must have left Duke Wayne feeling that his era was coming to a close. Perhaps that was an additional reason Duke had lobbied for the role. He understood this character, and he underplays it with skill and artistry.

※

It was a difficult shoot. Duke's earlier struggle with lung cancer had left him in a weakened state, apparent to the cast and crew of *The Shootist*. As it had during the filming of *True Grit* and *The Cowboys*, the high altitude of location shooting left him breathless. Everything seemed to exhaust him, and there was the added emotional burden of playing a role that so closely shadowed his own life. "Sometimes the irony of this film gets to me," he told a reporter. He quarreled often with Siegel and was ornery with his co-stars. "I knew he felt rotten all the time," Lauren Bacall later wrote in her 1994 memoir. " 'God, I can't smoke anymore, can't drink anymore, all the fun's gone!' " Duke complained to her during the shoot. But one day when a member of the crew exclaimed at the beauty of the day, Duke took Bacall's hand and said, "Every day you wake up is a beautiful day."

Books's—and Duke Wayne's—awareness that he is the last of a dying breed punctuates the film. When he first comes into town, he's disrespected by Cobb, who tells him to get out of the street and calls him "Methuselah." Marshal Thibido, in his unsuccessful bid to force him to leave town, tells Books that there's no place for a shootist like him in the new West, and he responds with glee at Books's cancer diagnosis. Books sees himself as a relic, and he looks for a place to die in peace.

As in *The Cowboys* and *True Grit*, Duke's character mentors a young man, one on the verge of going down the wrong path. In *The Shootist*, that's Gillom Rogers, the widow's teenage son, played winningly by Ron Howard in one of his first grown-up roles. Gillom works for the nasty Jay Cobb and, like Cobb, is interested mostly in drinking, fighting, and cussing. He's contemptuous of Books at first, agreeing with his boss that "the old man ain't worth a bullet. He looks all tuckered out." The latter observation Books agrees with; he readily admits to being weary. But when Gillom learns that Books is a famous gunman come to live under their roof, he is thrilled by the romance of Books's past exploits. When Books takes out three would-be assassins who attack him in his room, trying to make their names at his expense, Gillom is over the moon, while his mother is horrified, especially when her other boarders begin to leave. Books acts honorably toward her by offering to make up the financial loss caused by her departing boarders, and a genuine affection begins to develop between them despite her Christian qualms about the way he has conducted his life.

Gillom now dotes on the legendary shootist, and at one point Books offers to teach him something about guns, telling him that "a man should learn how to handle a gun and use it with discretion." It's the quintessential mentoring scene in many Westerns, though he's surprised to see that Gillom is already pretty good, having learned from the spiteful and intemperate Jay Cobb. But

＊

Duke Wayne and Lauren Bacall in Wayne's last film,
The Shootist, in 1976. Wayne's role as a gunslinger
dying of cancer was one of his greatest.

Books knows Gillom requires additional guidance, and he imparts his philosophy about what makes for victory in a gunfight. "It isn't always being fast," he tells the youth, "or even accurate, that counts. It's being *willing* . . . most men aren't. I am." He then tells Gillom, "There's more to being a man than the end of a gun," words that will reverberate by the end of the film. He also warns the boy to always be on the lookout for the unexpected, which is how most shootists meet their end.

Books thinks almost constantly about endings. He is searching for a way to die with dignity, not the bestial death described by Doc Hostetler. "A man's death is the most private thing in his life," he tells Bond Rogers, and in another powerful scene he says, "A man should be allowed his human dignity," spoken to an opportunistic ex-flame, Serepta, played by Sheree North, who wants to marry Books so she can make money selling his story to a pulp writer. "I'll not be remembered for a pack of lies," he tells her before throwing her out.

Books has made up his mind to go out on his own terms, in one final shoot-out with three bad men—Jay Cobb, Mike Sweeney, and Jack Pulford. He prepares to meet his death with the solemnity and dignity it deserves. He has the widow Rogers clean his best "Sunday-go-to-meeting" suit, which she does by sending it out for the new "process dry cleaning." He orders his epitaph, leaving off the death date but determined to die on his birthday. He has young Gillom get word to the three men to meet him at the Metropole Saloon, the fanciest watering hole in town, with the understanding that this will be their chance at a showdown with the legendary J. B. Books.

Siegel does a masterful job staging and filming the shoot-out in the Metropole, making good use of the outsized mirror over the bar, by which Books keeps his eye on all three of his opponents. That's how Swarthout envisioned and wrote the scene, and it makes for an elegant dance of precision and desperation among the four men. The hothead Jay Cobb draws first and is of course killed by Books. Then the vengeful Sweeney, older and more powerful but clouded by his desire to avenge a brother's death by Books's hand, shoots next, shielding himself with a saloon table. Books kills him, his bullets splintering the wood.

The most dangerous of the three—the cool, gun-proficient gambler Jack Pulford—wounds Books in his first shot and then stalks him, concealed by the long bar. Books, crouched behind the bar, is able to see Pulford reflected in a glass of whiskey and manages to kill him.

Gillom rushes in just in time to see the bartender—who doesn't have a dog in this fight but who shows up anyway, wielding a shotgun—fatally shoot Books in the back. He's the unexpected foe that Books had warned Gillom about. As the shootist lies dying on the barroom floor, Gillom picks up his gun and kills the bartender.

It's worth noting here that Duke made three important changes to this scene. First, in the novel and in the screen adaptation, Books orders a white wine when he first enters the bar. (What was Swarthout thinking?) Duke changed that to a whiskey. More important, the script called for Books to shoot Jay Cobb in the back. Duke vehemently objected. In the brief documentary on the making of *The Shootist*, Hugh O'Brian recalled Duke saying, "Wait a damn minute. I've done 265 films [*sic*]. I've never shot a man in the back and I don't intend to start now. You reshoot it or you get yourself another boy." The script also called for Gillom to shoot and kill Books, which would make him the next celebrated shootist. Again, Duke objected. Instead, Books looks imploringly at Gillom after he's killed the bartender, and Gillom—understanding the look in Books's eyes—throws the gun away. Books nods his approval in the moments before he dies.

According to Swarthout, the costumer Luster Bayless recalled that "John Wayne virtually dictated this new ending on the set when they shot it, telling director Siegel 'he would not compromise on this matter' and directing Ron Howard to throw Wayne's pistol as far away as possible, out of his life forever." One reason given was that he was afraid it would hurt Ron Howard's career—as he believed it had Bruce Dern's in *The Cowboys*—if he was seen killing John Wayne. Siegel wanted to film different endings and then audience test them, but Duke refused.

So what is to be made of John Wayne's final moments on-screen, in his valedictory film, after a lifetime of playing the unbeatable fighter and marksman, ending his career with what is essentially an antigun message? Film critic Carl Freedman compared him to Prospero in Shakespeare's *Tempest*—a farewell role in which he renounces his magic.

The wisdom that Duke's character imparts to young Gillom by word and by deed is the following: have courage, be willing, face the end with dignity, don't drink too much, don't cuss, and don't live by the gun. His role as a mentor has finally trumped his role as a shootist, a lesson sealed with his death.

"THE DUKE IS DEAD"

The Shootist turned out to be Duke's last picture, and it didn't do well at the box office, probably because of its somber theme. Frankovich recalled Paramount's head of marketing complaining, "Where are we gonna open this picture, hospitals?" The public did not want to see John Wayne weakened by cancer and facing his mortality. He himself garnered strong reviews in the role, however, because critics recognized the power of his understated performance. Arthur Knight wrote in the *Hollywood Reporter*, "Just when it seemed the Western was an endangered species . . . Wayne and Siegel have managed to validate it once more. *The Shootist* may well become a classic, ranking right up there with many of Wayne's earlier masterpieces." And Frank Rich, then writing for the *New York Post*, wrote, "Books is easily the star's best role in years. . . . Wayne makes a terminally ill character seem transcendentally alive."

In the years after *The Shootist*, Duke was too ill to work, except for a few commercials and two TV appearances: a special for General Electric and *Perry Como's Early American Christmas*, filmed in

Williamsburg, Virginia, in 1978. That same year, he endured open heart surgery to replace a defective mitral valve, and in 1979, three years after *The Shootist*, Wayne's cancer returned, this time in his stomach. On January 10, Duke's stomach was removed. The radiation treatments left him even weaker and struggling for control. He made his last public appearance two months before his death, at the 1979 Academy Awards ceremony at the Dorothy Chandler Pavilion in Los Angeles, to present the annual Best Picture Award. As some of Duke's biographers have noted, there was irony in his handing over the golden statuette to the producers of the anti–Vietnam War picture *The Deer Hunter*, a movie that stood in stark contrast to so much of what Duke had believed in, including the moral rightness of America's interventions.

And yet perhaps he had been able to come to terms with some of the radical changes that gripped America in the last two decades of his life: the refusal of many young men to fight in a war they saw as unjust, the blurring and breaking down of gender roles, the eroding of respect for law, order, and authority. Shortly before his death, Duke told a reporter, "Our country thrives on change. In nature nothing is permanent. So it stands to reason that as laws change, ideologies and mores change so that society changes, and that is good." Again, the real John Wayne might have been less rigid than his reputation, just as his best film roles were more nuanced, more loving, and sometimes more pacific than his iconic image would lead one to believe.

In June 1979, Duke entered UCLA Medical Center, where his cancer was discovered to have spread to his colon and throughout his lymph system. That's where he passed away, surrounded by his beloved children from his first and last marriages. Separated from Wayne since 1973, Pilar was unable to be with him when he passed away at 5:23 p.m. on June 11, 1979, discouraged from visiting by the grown children of his first marriage. He was seventy-two.

※

Which makes me think of my own father passing away in July 2006. Dad—Lieutenant Commander Sigmund B. Schoenberger—had always reminded me of John Wayne: his barrel chest and long legs, his self-reliance, a certain taciturn quality, his quiet devotion to his family of six kids, his willingness to teach us things, such as how to swim, how to fish, how to play softball, how to change the oil in your car. He even tried to teach my two oldest brothers how to box—a less than exuberant experiment that was never repeated. Trained as a navy fighter pilot in Korea, he named his Corsair the *Betty Ellen,* after our mother.

At the end, he had suffered small strokes and complications from peripheral neuropathy that left him, in his final year, bedridden in a nursing home in Pensacola, Florida, where he and my mother had retired because that's where he had attended test pilot school, decades earlier, as an ensign in the navy. Virtually paralyzed, this once proud and active man was totally reliant on health-care workers—all of them amazing, patient folks—to take care of his most basic needs. Because his mind remained sharp, he got through this yearlong ordeal because Betty came every day to read to him his favorite novel, Larry McMurtry's great Western, *Lonesome Dove.* And my brother Jack came every night to watch movies with him.

What movies did they watch? Westerns, of course. Not all John Wayne–John Ford Westerns, because Dad was also a big fan of Randolph Scott, but John Wayne movies figured prominently in getting my dad through his ordeal of being a prisoner of his own body, as though he were a prisoner of war. So much of John Wayne's persona resonated with how my father had lived his life, including Wayne's role in non-Westerns like the 1953 aviation classic, William Wellman's *Island in the Sky*, in which Wayne portrayed a pilot stranded with his crew in a frozen wasteland in Quebec. We find out at the end of the film why he is so eager to survive and return home: he has six children, like Dad. While he was stranded in his own wasteland, to see his hero reflect his own life choices must have given Dad some comfort, and affirmation, at the end of his days.

Future generations of men won't conform to the John Wayne mold cut by John Ford, and perhaps the absence of Ford and Wayne from the cultural stage is more of a loss than we realize. Many of the lessons they had to teach still ring true to contemporary ears. I think some of the confusion today about masculinity stems from the fact that we no longer grow up watching Westerns, which are parables of (mostly) men trying to do the right thing. The Western hero, as Ford and Wayne imagined him, grapples with moral as well as physical dilemmas. He mentors the young. The Fordian hero is capable of admitting he's wrong and is capable of saying he's sorry. He looks after and protects those weaker than himself and respects those—even women—who can carry their own weight. In other incarnations, notably Matt Dillon in *Gunsmoke*, the Western hero practices a kind of gun control—taking guns away from predators and miscreants and sometimes banning them from town. The Western hero respects women, even if he seldom gets the girl, because Westerns are really morality tales and not romances.

In the deeply satisfying guise of the quest or adventure narrative, often against the backdrop of starkly beautiful American vistas, to the pleasing sound of hoofbeats and vernacular American song, Westerns seduce us into seeing how mere mortals become heroes, how boys become men.

Acknowledgments

First and foremost, I thank Dan Ford for allowing me to peruse the
John Ford Papers, the impressive archive he was instrumental in
assembling, housed at Indiana University's Lilly Library, and giving
me permission to quote from unpublished material. I'm also grateful
for the help extended to me by Lilly Library's research librarians and
by my research assistant, Joseph Hiland, who was inspired to write
about the great stuntmen who toiled in the Westerns of John Ford
and John Wayne. The Lilly Library's Everett Helm Visiting Fellow-
ship allowed me to immerse myself in the archive, and for that, my
thanks.

I am ever grateful that the luminescent Maureen O'Hara granted
me an interview a few years before she passed away, in the enchant-
ing seaside town of Glengarriff in the Republic of Ireland, where
she spent many of her final years. I'll never forget dining with Miss
O'Hara at Casey's Hotel—with her helpers and companions, Marie,
Carolyn, Geraldine, Carol—and hearing her sing that heartbreaking
Irish anthem "Kevin Barry." Thanks also to Casey Hotel's genial pro-
prietor, Donal Deasy, who helped make the evening possible, seating
us in her usual corner table by a wood-burning furnace that added
warmth to a rainy April evening.

I'm grateful, too, to the director and film historian Peter Bogdanovich, for his deep scholarship, insights, and appreciation of both John Ford and John Wayne. He generously gave of his time to talk with me about Ford Westerns—especially *The Man Who Shot Liberty Valance*. He is probably the last man standing who knew both men and loved their work.

Nancy Gray, my friend and colleague at The College of William & Mary, read early versions of this book and gave me invaluable suggestions and resources. Thanks also to another valued colleague, Varun Begley, for conversations about Howard Hawks's *Red River*, and to my nephew Joshua Day—a gifted writer!—who read early chapters and encouraged me to go further. And to my spouse, Sam Kashner, for his countless kindnesses, insights, and encouragement.

William & Mary helped support the writing of this book through an academic research leave and through a Plumeri Award for Faculty Excellence, administered by the college and endowed by the philanthropist Joseph Plumeri—a game guy and a knowledgeable fan of Ford-Wayne Westerns!

Finally, my thanks to my agent David Kuhn, to Sarah Levitt and Nicole Tourtelot at Kuhn Projects for their guidance, and to my publisher and editor, the legendary Nan Talese. I have lived much with legends lately.

Sources

ARCHIVES

John Ford Papers, Lilly Library, University of Indiana, Bloomington.

ARTICLES

Begley, Varun. "'One Right Guy to Another': Howard Hawks and Auteur Theory Revisited." *Camera Obscura* 64 (2007).

Bennett, Jessica. "Man Deconstructed." *New York Times*, Aug. 9, 2015.

Bogdanovich, Peter. "The Duke's Gone West." *New York*, June 25, 1979.

Bolger, Daniel P. "The Truth About the Wars." *New York Times*, Nov. 11, 2014.

Bosworth, Patricia. "John Wayne, Larger than Life." In *John Wayne: The Legend and the Man*. Brooklyn: Powerhouse Books, 2012.

Didion, Joan. "John Wayne: A Love Song." In *Slouching Towards Bethlehem*. New York: Pocket Books, 1968.

Freedman, Carl. "Post-heterosexuality: John Wayne and the Construction of American Masculinity." www.filmint.nu.

Haskell, Molly. "Wayne, Westerns, and Women." *Ladies' Home Journal*, July 1976.

Kehr, David. "John Ford, on Uncommon Ground." *New York Times*, Nov. 10, 2013.

———. "John Ford's Portraits of Loss and Redemption." *New York Times*, Feb. 10, 2013.

Kimmel, Michael S. "Masculinity as Homophobia." In *Sex, Gender, and Sexuality: The New Basics*, edited by Abby L. Ferber, Kimberly Holcomb, and Tre Wentling. New York: Oxford University Press, 2009.

Lethem, Jonathan. "The Darkest Side of John Wayne." *Salon*, Aug. 11, 1997.

McMurtry, Larry, and Diana Ossana. "Talking About 'True Grit.'" http://www.nybooks.com/blogs/nyrblog/2011/feb/08/.

Miller, Claire Cain. "A Disadvantaged Start in Life Harms Boys More than Girls." *New York Times*, Oct. 22, 2015.

Scott, A. O. "The Post-Man." *New York Times Magazine*, Nov. 10, 2013.

Wallace, Chris. "Mythic Middle-Aged Protectors." *New York Times*, March 8, 2015.

Weiss, Bari. "Camille Paglia: A Feminist Defense of Masculine Virtues." www.wsj.com/news/article, Dec. 28, 2013.

BOOKS

Anderson, Lindsay. *About John Ford*. London: Plexus, 1981, 1999.

Bacall, Lauren. *Now*. New York: Alfred A. Knopf, 1994.

Bogdanovich, Peter. *John Ford*. Berkeley: University of California Press, 1978.

———. *Picture Shows: Peter Bogdanovich on the Movies*. London: George Allen & Unwin, 1975.

———. *Who the Hell's in It*. New York: Alfred A. Knopf, 2004.

Canutt, Yakima. *Stunt Man*. With Oliver Drake. New York: Walker, 1979.

Carey, Harry, Jr. *Company of Heroes: My Life as an Actor in the John Ford Stock Company*. Metuchen, N.J.: Scarecrow Press, 1994.

Davis, Ronald L. *Duke: The Life and Image of John Wayne*. Norman: University of Oklahoma Press, 1998.

———. *John Ford: Hollywood's Old Master*. Norman: University of Oklahoma Press, 1995.

Donovan, Jack. *The Way of Men*. Milwaukie, Ore.: Dissonant Hum, 2012.

Exley, Jo Ella Powell. *Frontier Blood: Saga of the Parker Family*. College Station: Texas A&M University Press, 2001.

Eyman, Scott. *John Wayne: The Life and Legend*. New York: Simon & Schuster, 2014.

———. *Print the Legend: The Life and Times of John Ford*. Baltimore: Johns Hopkins University Press, 1999.

Ford, Dan. *Pappy: The Life of John Ford*. New York: Da Capo Press, 1998.

Frankel, Glenn. *The Searchers: The Making of an American Legend*. London: Bloomsbury, 2013.

Gallagher, Tag. *John Ford: The Man and His Films*. Berkeley: University of California Press, 1986.

Harris, Mark. *Five Came Back: A Story of Hollywood and the Second World War*. New York: Penguin Press, 2014.

Haskell, Molly. *From Reverence to Rape: The Treatment of Women in the Movies*. 2nd ed. Chicago: University of Chicago Press, 1987.

Leaming, Barbara. *Katharine Hepburn*. New York: Crown, 1995.

Mast, Gerald. *Howard Hawks, Storyteller*. Oxford: Oxford University Press, 1982.

McBride, Joseph. *Searching for John Ford*. New York: St. Martin's Griffin, 2003.

Mellen, Joan. *Big Bad Wolves: Masculinity in the American Film*. New York: Pantheon Books, 1977.

Munn, Michael. *John Wayne: The Man Behind the Myth*. New York: New American Library, 2005.

O'Brien, Darcy. *A Way of Life, Like Any Other*. New York: *New York Review of Books*, 1977.

O'Hara, Maureen. *'Tis Herself: An Autobiography*. With John Nicoletti. New York: Simon & Schuster, 2004.

Peary, Gerald, and Jenny Lefcourt, eds. *John Ford Interviews*. Jackson: University Press of Mississippi, 2001.

Pippin, Robert B. *Hollywood Westerns and American Myth: The Importance of Howard Hawks and John Ford for Political Philosophy*. New Haven, Conn.: Yale University Press, 2010.

Ricci, Mark, Boris Zmijewsky, and Steve Zmijewsky. *The Films of John Wayne*. New York: Citadel Press, 1970.

Sarris, Andrew. *The American Cinema: Directors and Directions, 1929–1968*. Chicago: University of Chicago Press, 1985.

———. *The John Ford Movie Mystery*. Bloomington: Indiana University Press, 1975.

———, ed. *Interviews with Film Directors*. New York: Bobbs-Merrill, 1967.

Shepherd, Donald, Robert Slatzer, and Dave Grayson. *Duke: The Life and Times of John Wayne*. New York: Citadel Press, 2002.

Swarthout, Miles. Introduction to *The Shootist*, by Glendon Swarthout. Lincoln: University of Nebraska Press, 2011.

Tompkins, Jane. *West of Everything: The Inner Life of Westerns*. Oxford: Oxford University Press, 1992.

Wayne, Aissa. *John Wayne, My Father*. With Steve Delsohn. Lanham, Md.: Taylor Trade, 1998.

Wayne, Pilar. *John Wayne: My Life with the Duke*. With Alex Thorleifson. New York: McGraw-Hill, 1987.

Wills, Garry. *John Wayne's America: The Politics of Celebrity*. New York: Simon & Schuster, 1997.

DOCUMENTARIES AND FEATURETTES

The Battle of Midway, directed by John Ford. U.S. Navy–20th Century Fox, 1942.

Becoming John Ford, directed by Nick Redman. The Ford at Fox Collection DVD.

The Breaking of Boys and the Making of Men, with director Mark Rydell. Warner Bros. Deluxe Edition.

The Cowboys, Together Again, with director Mark Rydell. Warner Bros. Deluxe Edition.

Directed by John Ford, directed by Peter Bogdanovich.

The Great American West of John Ford. Synergy Entertainment.

John Ford/John Wayne: The Filmmaker & the Legend. American Masters special feature included in Warner Bros. Special Edition of *Stagecoach*.

The Man Who Shot Liberty Valance. Featurette, The John Wayne Collection, Warner Video.

The Shootist, Cast and Crew Interviews. Warner Home Video.

Stagecoach: A Story of Redemption. Special feature. Warner Home Video, Special Edition of *Stagecoach*.

A Turning of the Earth: John Ford, John Wayne, and "The Searchers." 1998. Narrated by John Milius. The John Wayne Collection, Warner Video.

FEATURE FILMS (LISTED CHRONOLOGICALLY)

The Iron Horse, 1924. The Ford at Fox Collection DVD.

The Big Trail, 1930. 20th Century Fox Special Edition.

Stagecoach, 1939. Warner Home Video Special Edition.

Fort Apache, 1948. The John Wayne Collection, RKO Radio Pictures.

3 Godfathers, 1948. Metro-Goldwyn-Mayer, Warner Home Video.

Red River, 1948. United Artists, MGM Home Entertainment.

She Wore a Yellow Ribbon, 1949. Turner Home Entertainment.

Rio Grande, 1950. Republic Pictures. Olive Pictures DVD.

The Searchers, 1956. Warner Video.

The Man Who Shot Liberty Valance, 1962. Paramount Pictures. The John Wayne Collection, Warner Video.

True Grit, 1969. Paramount Home Entertainment.

The Cowboys, 1972. Universal Pictures, Warner Bros. Deluxe Edition.

The Shootist, 1976. Paramount Pictures, Warner Home Video.

Notes

PROLOGUE: WHY WESTERNS STILL MATTER

1   "John Ford and John Wayne taught us": *John Ford/John Wayne: The Filmmaker & the Legend*, documentary.

1   "I've played the kind of man": Wayne quoted in Eyman, *John Wayne*, 565.

1   "It is easy to see why so few women": Wills, *John Wayne's America*, 157.

2   "When John Wayne rode": Joan Didion, "John Wayne, a Love Song," *Slouching Towards Bethlehem*, 44.

2   Wayne's 136th picture: There are varying accounts of Wayne's total film count; I'm using Davis's filmography in *Duke*.

2   "Saw the walk": Didion, "John Wayne, a Love Song," 44.

2   "I am here": Haskell, "Wayne, Westerns, and Women," 77.

2   "We rode the range": Ibid., 94.

3   "the father figure": Ibid., 92.

3   "[He] was paternal": Ibid., 94.

3   "doesn't immediately see her": Ibid.

4   "Masculinity is just becoming something": Weiss, "Camille Paglia."

5   "Boys get a message": Quoted in Miller, "Disadvantaged Start in Life Harms Boys More than Girls."

5   "What other American icon": Lethem, "Darkest Side of John Wayne."

CHAPTER 1: BIRTH OF THE WESTERN HERO

9   "Nobody should come to the movies": Wayne, quoted in Davis, *Duke*, 14.

9   "When I pass on": *John Ford/John Wayne: The Filmmaker & the Legend*.

9   "the essence of classical American cinema": Ibid.
9   "I had an eye for composition": Ibid.
10   "Ford's movies are visual ballads": Ibid.
10   "He wasn't portraying": Ibid.
10   "From roughly 1900 to 1975": Tompkins, *West of Everything*, 5.
12   "The desert light": Ibid., 4.
12   Writers on sex, gender, and sexuality: Kimmel, "Masculinity as Homo-
     phobia," 61.
12   "men prove their manhood": Ibid.
13   " 'No Sissy Stuff' ": Ibid., 62.
13   "Many movie stars": Freedman, "Post-heterosexuality," 19.
18   "when men compete": Donovan, *Way of Men*, 2.

CHAPTER 2: THE GOOD BAD MAN

24   "Dammit. The son of a bitch looked like a man": Walsh quoted in
     Didion, "John Wayne: A Love Song," 45.
24   "To live outside the law you must be honest": Bob Dylan, "Absolutely
     Sweet Marie."
25   "remarkable quality of innocence": Bogdanovich, "Duke's Gone
     West," 67.
25   "Duke wasn't ready": John Ford interview, John Ford Papers (hereaf-
     ter cited as JFP), Lilly Library.
27   "I met Duke": Ibid.
27   "I had no ambition": John Wayne interview, JFP.
27   "When I went back to school": Ibid.
28   "We were between San Diego": Ibid.
28   "I should have complained": Frankel, *Searchers*, 228.
31   "He had a good height": Walsh quoted in ibid.
31   "Yeah. He wanted a name": Ford interview, JFP.
32   "I like[d] Duke's style": Ibid.
33   "I remember he was evidently": Wayne interview, JFP.
34   "calculated to appeal": Davis, *Duke*, 48.
34   "Keep your goddamn fly buttoned": Ibid.
35   "a drunk and a rebel": Ibid., 49.
35   "For a year I couldn't get work": Ibid.
35   "Most of the company": Ibid., 51.
36   "Wayne got to be terrific": Ibid., 57.
36   "a goddamn pansy": Ibid.
37   "projected a quality": Ibid., 83.
37   "I made up my mind": Ibid., 58.
37   "When I started, I knew": Wayne interview, JFP.
37   "Pappy was full of bullshit": Ford, *Pappy*, 138.
39   "The truth about my life": Davis, *John Ford*, 19.
39   "Ford's famous act": *Becoming John Ford*, documentary.

40   "I am of the proletariat": Davis, *John Ford*, 19.
40   "one great emotional tragedy": Ibid., 16.
41   "Pop was responsible": Carey, *Company of Heroes*, 45.
41   "Roaming the mountains": Ibid., 47.
41   "He and my father": Ibid.
42   "natural and rugged": Davis, *John Ford*, 38.
42   "He won't ask me": Carey, *Company of Heroes*, 2.
43   "buried himself in work": Davis, *John Ford*, 48.
44   "Duke describe[d] how Ford": *Becoming John Ford*, documentary.
45   "or one of the local whorehouses": Davis, *Duke*, 63.
45   "I never expected anything from Jack": Wayne interview, JFP.
46   "I'm having a hell of a time": Davis, *Duke*, 81.
47   "You idiot. Couldn't you play it?": Ibid.
47   "When the time came": Ford interview, JFP.
50   "What already counts for the Wayne character": Mellen, *Big Bad Wolves*, 135.
53   "at the bend in the river": Didion, "John Wayne, a Love Story," 44.
54   "I myself am a pretty ugly fellow": *Becoming John Ford*, documentary.
55   "They were all hard drinkers": Mary Ford interview, JFP.
55   "Why are you moving your mouth": Davis, *Duke*, 83.
57   "When we first started *Stagecoach*": Wayne interview, JFP.
57   "Jack Ford stood up for me": Ibid.
57   "You are a big, dumb": Davis, *Duke*, 88.

CHAPTER 3: SOLDIER'S JOY: THE CAVALRY TRILOGY
64   "To me he was sort of like Moses": McDowall quoted in Davis, *John Ford*, 159.
64   "In the military, we love our legends": Bolger, "Truth About the Wars."
64   "Gimme some of that Soldier's Joy": "Soldier's Joy, 1864," lyrics by Guy Clark.
65   "The Japanese shrimp fleet": Ford, quoted in Davis, *John Ford*, 155.
66   "Ford just loved it!": Ibid., 158–59.
67   "The thing that sticks out": Ibid., 159.
69   "Their experiences during the war": Harris, *Five Came Back*, 440.
70   "My father was an absolute": Davis, *John Ford*, 204.
70   "the writer had better keep": Ibid., 205.
71   "on the frontier, the troops": Ibid., 223.
71   "Masculinity is about being a man": Donovan, *Way of Men*, 2.
75   "poetic" and "beautiful": Davis, *John Ford*, 52.
76   "I wouldn't give that son of a bitch": Ibid., 211.
77   "I literally saw tears": Ibid., 209.
83   "really didn't relate to women": Davis, *John Ford*, 224.
85   "My grandfather's macho image": Davis, *John Ford*, 206.
86   "The Navajo loved it": Ibid.

87   "The real star of my Westerns": Ibid., 205–6.
87   "That's how he kept people on their toes": Ibid., 209.
88   "Here [we] were in the middle of the West": Ibid., 242.
88   "Duke used to talk about": Ibid., 227.
88   "Ford was the type of person": Ibid.
89   "Ford liked to watch me ride a horse": Ibid., 224.
90   "I learned to react, not to act": Munn, *John Wayne: The Man Behind the Myth*, 48.
90   "the greatest guy I ever knew": O'Hara, interview with author.
92   "The usual gang was there": O'Hara, *'Tis Herself*, 103–4.
93   "There were times when you": O'Hara, interview with author.
93   "a miniature Monument Valley": Davis, *John Ford*, 234.
94   "A lot of the Irish went west": Ibid., 207.
95   "I've been able to ride a horse": Ibid., 227.
96   "Hey, stupid": Bogdanovich, interview with author.
96   "He knew he'd been wrong": Carey, *Company of Heroes*, 121.
96   "Ford loved drunks": Davis, *John Ford*, 231.
98   "He's always eatin' on a handkerchief": Ibid., 235.
98   "All right, go at it!": Carey, *Company of Heroes*, 188–89.
100   "my nature, my religion": *Becoming John Ford*, documentary.

CHAPTER 4: THE AVENGING LONER: THE SEARCHERS
102   "I didn't know that the big": McBride, *Searching for John Ford*, 459–60.
105   "the most iconic way": Bogdanovich, interview with author.
106   "was always underrated": *Becoming John Ford*, documentary.
108   "one of the most beautiful films": Ibid.
111   "safeguard the perimeter": Donovan, *Way of Men*, 1–3.
114   "I am convinced that the white people did more harm": Tom Champion, quoted in Jo Ella Powell Exley, *Frontier Blood: Saga of the Parker Family*, 176.
115   "Ethan Edwards is not a villain": *Becoming John Ford*, documentary.
117   "the audience doesn't hate him": Bogdanovich, interview with author.
118   "tribalism": *Searching for John Ford*, documentary.
120   "picturing the complicated face of racism": Bogdanovich, interview with author.
121   "community, tradition, ritual": Ibid.
122   "peace and acceptance": *Becoming John Ford*, documentary.
124   "the eternal outsider": Bogdanovich, interview with author.

CHAPTER 5: LOVE AND POLITICS
127   "I was dancing barefoot": Davis, *Duke*, 166–67.
127   "Like many fine artists": Davis, *John Ford*, 8.
128   "If you don't live up to it": Pilar Wayne, *John Wayne*, 43.
128   "I was America to them": Davis, *Duke*, 114.

128 "You know, our most decorated soldier": Hartmann, quoted in ibid., 119.
129 "bully John Wayne": Ibid., 117.
130 "He would become a 'super patriot'": Pilar Wayne, *John Wayne*, 43.
130 "A great, pale jungle moon": Davis, *Duke*, 167.
131 "in fact . . . a high-class call girl": Pilar Wayne, *John Wayne*, 170.
131 "Anyway I don't give a four letter word": Davis, *Duke*, 109.
131 "Duke . . . walked away": Ibid., 110.
133 "My husband is one of the few persons": Ibid., 124.
133 "physical and mental cruelty": Ibid., 168.
134 "It was an embarrassing ordeal": Davis, *Duke*, 178–79.
134 "To me, [Hispanic women] seem more warm": Wayne quoted in ibid., 186.
135 "until they were ready to rot": Leaming, *Katharine Hepburn*, 305–6.
136 "His family life was terrible": *The Man Who Shot Liberty Valance*, featurette.
136 "Well, Ma, I sure fell in love": John Ford to Mary Ford, JFP.
136 "The only things I miss": Ibid.
137 "find a manlier occupation": Leaming, *Katharine Hepburn*, 328.
137 "Abuse poured constantly": Ibid., 312.
137 "a little frightened": Ibid., 310.
137 "the more successful he became": Ibid., 312.
137 "three drops of juniper juice": Ibid., 310.
138 "Fearful of intimacy": Davis, *John Ford*, 8–9.
138 "was not, for instance, homophobic": Eyman, *Print the Legend*, 21.
138 "poked fun at Ford's 'infatuation'": McBride, *Searching for John Ford*, 121.
139 "This may have been the first time": Ibid.
139 "the gossip about Jack's masculinity": Ibid., 122.
139 "I walked into his office": O'Hara, *'Tis Herself*, 190.
140 "the separate bedrooms": Ibid., 190–91.
140 "It was the fourth picture": Ibid., 187–88.
140 "Well, did Herself": Ibid., 188.
140 "His fantasies and crushes": Ibid., 191.
141 "Father—I love my man dearly": Ibid.
141 "still in Bel Air before he moved": Bogdanovich, interview with author.
142 "like a fella": McBride, *Searching for John Ford*, 451.
142 "an unquenchable need": Davis, *John Ford*, 9.
143 "We make out of the quarrel": John Butler Yeats, *Anima Hominis*.
144 "Ah, go on!": Davis, *John Ford*, 162.
145 "I don't think there is anyone": Ibid., 244.
146 "undaunted by the vicious campaign": PR for *Big Jim McLain*.
148 "One wonders about the future": Quoted in Davis, *Duke*, 166.
148 "Whether he went overboard": Ibid.

CHAPTER 6: LOST BATTLES

152 "That picture lost so much money": Quoted in Davis, *Duke*, 233.

152 "Well, Wayne was the central character": Bogdanovich, interview with author.

154 "He ate, slept, and dreamed that picture": Patrick Wayne quoted in Davis, *Duke*, 224.

156 "had always been growly with us": Roberson, quoted in Davis, *John Ford*, 298.

157 "It was the first time": Ford quoted in ibid.

157 "I hope to go to Texas": Davis, *Duke*, 227.

157 "Jesus Christ, Duke": Ibid.

158 "I don't think we used three cuts": Ibid., 228.

158 "He had put every penny": Ibid., 227.

160 "It will last forever, run forever": Ibid., 231.

160 "I have great affection": Ibid., 233.

161 "reawaken American patriotism": Ibid., 220.

161 "response to all the flag burners": Ibid.

162 "death was more than a dismal abstract": Ibid., 235.

162 "The Hero Doesn't Win": *The Man Who Shot Liberty Valance*, featurette.

163 "I'd worked twenty years for no gain": Davis, *Duke*, 234.

163 "I was scared to death": Wayne quoted in Munn, *John Wayne*, 231.

163 "I'll tell you why I love her": Davis, *Duke*, 238.

163 " 'If I don't make this movie' ": Aissa Wayne, *John Wayne, My Father*, 47.

164 "looked more like photography": *Directed by John Ford*, documentary.

164 "There was one reason": Munn, *John Wayne*, 232.

164 "Ford was a complete bastard": Ibid., 233.

166 "How many times did you risk": Ibid., 234.

166 "was in a foul mood": Ibid., 232.

166 "rode Wayne so hard": Ibid., 214.

166 "He beat up on Duke": Bogdanovich, interview with author.

168 "Jimmy, you are not a coward": *Directed by John Ford*, documentary.

171 "Heroes Don't Brag": Sign outside a U.S. Navy SEAL recruiting center in Chattanooga. *New York Times*, July 21, 2015.

172 "It's one of the most ironic lines": Bogdanovich, interview with author.

172 "Well, Wayne was the central character": Ibid.

172 "It's his last word on the West": Ibid.

172 "It's a haunted film": *Liberty Valance*, featurette.

CHAPTER 7: JOURNEY TO MANHOOD:
TEACHING THE NEXT GENERATION

174 "He could never forgive himself": Davis, *Duke*, 262.

174 "If you give me the chance": *The Breaking of Boys and the Making of Men*, featurette.

174   "wrestle with the little pups": *New York Times*, June 6, 2015.

175   "His constant coughing": Pilar Wayne, *John Wayne*, 180.

176   "I knew Duke was very sick": Ibid., 177.

176   "neither of us was able to say the word": Ibid., 178.

176   "you'll never work again": Ibid., 179.

176   "Duke wasn't sure": Ibid.

177   "He is like a son": Ibid., 185.

178   the best screenplay he had ever read: Shepherd, Slatzer, and Grayson, *Duke*.

178   "I was weaned on stories": "Marguerite Roberts," http://m.imdb.com/name/nm0731387/quotes.

178   "There was a kind of beauty": Davis, *Duke*, 286–87.

184   "Wow! . . . If I'd known what": Ibid., 291.

184   "the story of *True Grit*": McMurtry and Ossana, "Talking About 'True Grit,'" 1.

184   "The political John Wayne never showed up": *The Breaking of Boys*, featurette.

185   "If you give me the chance": Ibid.

185   "He *wanted* it": Ibid.

185   "He loved being pushed": Ibid.

185   "John Wayne was a very impressive": Ibid.

186   "felt he raised his acting level": Ibid.

186   "Jack Ford treated me like that": Ibid.

187   "country boys": Ibid.

187   "thrilled to have the opportunity": Ibid.

187   "the greatest experience of my life": Ibid.

188   "He was very paternal and very loving": Ibid.

188   "Anyone who's ever directed": Ibid.

189   "America will hate you": Ibid.

189   "It was hard on him": Ibid.

189   "One could easily think that Warner Bros.": Pauline Kael, *New Yorker*, Jan. 2, 1972, 83.

191   "The picture has a legendary quality": *Breaking of Boys*, featurette.

192   "Wayne loved the script": Ibid.

CHAPTER 8: GOING WEST: TWILIGHT OF THE GODS

193   "I have a lust for . . . dignity": Davis, *Duke*, 238.

193   "I've long wanted to do a story": Davis, *John Ford*, 321.

194   "That's when the whole thing": Ibid., 326.

195   "Let's do the goddamn thing": Ibid., 331.

195   "I don't like porn": Ibid., 335.

196   "Come for the death watch": Leaming, *Katharine Hepburn*, 505.

196   "I love you": Bogdanovich, interview with author.

197   "He was Irish": Hepburn on *The Dick Cavett Show*, Oct. 26, 1973.

197 "As soon as Wayne had the lead": Miles Swarthout, introduction to *The Shootist*, by Glendon Swarthout, ix.

198 "It's the kind of picture": Davis, *Duke*, 315.

201 "Sometimes the irony of this film": Ibid.

201 "I knew he felt rotten": Bacall, *Now*.

201 " 'God, I can't smoke anymore' ": Davis, *Duke*, 316.

205 "Wait a damn minute": O'Brian quoted in *The Shootist*, Cast and Crew Interviews.

205 "John Wayne virtually dictated": Swarthout, introduction to *The Shootist*, xxi.

206 "The Duke Is Dead": *L.A. Herald Examiner*, June 12, 1979.

206 "Where are we gonna open": Swarthout, introduction to *The Shootist*, xvi.

206 "Just when it seemed": Ibid., xvii.

206 "Books is easily the star's": Ibid., xviii.

207 "Our country thrives on change": Davis, *Duke*, 328.

Index

Page numbers in *italics* refer to illustrations.

Nancy Schoenberger is a professor of English and director of creative writing at The College of William & Mary. She is the author of *Dangerous Muse: The Life of Lady Caroline Blackwood* and co-author, with her husband, Sam Kashner, of books on Oscar Levant, George Reeves, and the love affair, marriages, and working relationship of Elizabeth Taylor and Richard Burton. The author of three award-winning books of poetry, Schoenberger divides her time between Williamsburg, Virginia, and New York City.

A NOTE ON THE TYPE

This book was set in a typeface called Berling. This distinguished let-ter is a computer version of the original type designed by the Swedish typographer Karl-Erik Forsberg (1914–1995). Forsberg is also known for designing several other typefaces, including Parad (1936), Lunda (1938), Carolus, and Ericus, but Berling—named after the foundry that produced it, Berlingska Stilgjuteriet of Lund—is the one for which he is best known. Berling, a roman font with the characteristics of an old face, was first used to produce *The Rembrandt Bible* in 1954, which won an award for the most beautiful book of the year.